Arts in Education

THE MAKING OF A GRASS BLADE

Barbara Carlisle, Author

Published by the W. K. Kellogg Foundation

Battle Creek, Michigan

Library of Congress Catalog Card Number: 89 -063224
Printed in the United States of America

W. K. Kellogg Foundation
400 North Avenue
Battle Creek, Michigan
49017–3398

March 1990

CONTENTS

About the Author

Barbara Carlisle's career in the arts and theater has encompassed teaching, consulting, choreography, playwriting, and arts education curriculum design.

Mrs. Carlisle received her doctorate degree in art history from the University of Michigan, Ann Arbor and in 1977 became coordinator of all arts programs for the Michigan Department of Education. She later studied in China with a team of art educators, and prepared a comparative study of Chinese and American art.

A professional director of community theater for the past 15 years, Mrs. Carlisle has directed plays at the Cincinnati Playhouse in the Park, and at the Boarshead Theatre in Lansing, Michigan. She also writes theatre pieces, and is currently an associate professor of Theatre Arts at Virginia Tech University, Blacksburg.

When the Kellogg Foundation began its Arts in Michigan Education program, Mrs. Carlisle served as a consultant to design its format and monitor its progress. Her experience in working closely with schools and art organizations gave her an excellent perspective on the intricacies of collaborative arts education programming.

Foreword

Affordable, innovative options are needed for curriculum and school planners, organizations, and civic leaders who want to see the arts education remain alive and well — for tomorrow's young people.

For the W. K. Kellogg Foundation, the series of arts projects covered in this book was a special initiative. The Foundation does not ordinarily fund programs in the arts. The Michigan Arts Program was unique, was conducted only in the Foundation's home state, and is likely to remain unique in future programming priorities.

But the lessons learned and the concepts that unfolded carry long-range and positive options. In the following pages are details about the *concepts* for designing a dozen special arts-related projects. Their successes are described, their shortfalls are illuminated. The intent is to provide sufficient data to enable readers to adapt, emulate, and improvise on the concepts in order to develop worthwhile, doable programs in their communities.

Early in this book the author writes that "the loss of arts in the schools threatens to reduce the effectiveness of education in general and *endangers the future of many young people in particular.*" A strong contention if it is accurate, its ramifications are deep and wide. It could mean, if true, that students of all ages and interests may find diminished personal fulfillment in his or her classroom years.

What those circumstances will do to the professional and personal developmental conditions of the student is unknown. Some people, such as this book's author, believe it will *endanger* the student's future and "the future of our culture."

If you share that concern and want to do something about it, read on. You just may find your answer.

Norman A. Brown, President, W. K. Kellogg Foundation

The Arts...the Discovery... the Connection.

A Guide to Program Development for Arts in Education

We all were taken there on buses, to a great hall, where thousands of other children just like us were herded down the narrow aisles, the noise of our chatter reverberating through the giant auditorium. On the stage a field of men and women, dressed in black, made random horn and string noises to add to the din. Then, suddenly, cued by hisses from the older children...the buzzing of the children stopped. Far down on the stage a man in a long swallowtail coat stepped in front of the orchestra. It became quiet. All of us waited, barely breathing, while he tapped the stand and lifted his white baton. The music began with a roar, catching our childish cynicism off guard. Without being told, we knew this was not the stuff you heard on the radio or the record player. This was real music made by people we could see, now, just for us. In some way we entered a new world and made a discovery that would last a lifetime. When we went the next year, and the next, we would initiate the younger children into the rituals, confident in our worldliness.

And so we came to know "Peter and the Wolf," "The Carnival of the Animals," the waltzes of Strauss and Brahms, the marches of Sousa, "The Pines and Fountains of Rome," "Eine Kleine Nacht Music," and all those "first pieces" that lead to others, and still others.

In the same auditorium, one year we saw "Mrs. Wiggs and the Cabbage Patch"; another time, "Puss in Boots"; and the next year we clapped with all our power to bring back "Tinker Bell" for Wendy and Peter Pan. Not far down the street was the Art Museum where we moved in small packs from one mysterious dark painting to another, the back row elbowing its way forward to hear a lady explaining in hushed tones who those strangely dressed ladies and gentlemen from the past were.

These memories of childhood visits to the great arts institutions of our towns and cities are treasures that have become rarer and rarer. Schools have cut back their field trips because of curriculum demands, the rising cost of buses, the disappearance of aides and chaperones, or simply, the cost of entrance fees. In small towns and far out in the country, the time and travel have always been prohibitive. Arts organizations have had to allocate their tight budgets to rent, production materials, insurance, and all the escalating costs of operating any institution. Consequently, their education programs have been reduced.

There have also been problems with those surviving programs.

Events of all kinds have been planned without the age and attention span of the young people in mind. Scheduling has been more of an interruption than a help to the teacher. Some teachers have been indifferent to the programs and have given the children no idea of the purpose or nature of the events.

Sometimes one set of children has received all the benefits and nothing has been planned for the rest of the students. In other cases the performance space has been simply too large or too small. Sometimes performing groups have come in and left a school in such a hurry that hardly anyone knew what had happened. In other cases groups have arrived with one set of expectations and the schools have had another. Performers have been oblivious to the demands of school schedules. Schools have failed to give the artist appropriate space or a teacher to help with discipline.

All of these problems have diminished the enthusiasm of both the arts organizations and the schools for cooperative planning.

A Search for Solutions

The Michigan Arts and Education Program of the W. K. Kellogg Foundation began officially with its announcement at the Detroit Institute of Arts on

February 24, 1983. The program had been in planning for more than 18 months by that time. Its two goals were to strengthen the arts programming for school-aged children of the state's major arts institutions, and to assist those arts organizations with their general well-being. The program came on the scene at a time when Michigan's economy was severely stressed, a condition reflected in reduced or eliminated arts curricula in the schools themselves and in stringent budgeting for all the professional arts organizations of the state. The guidelines of the Kellogg program were devised to support major organizations who could devote serious attention to bringing arts experiences to children in school and who could demonstrate competency in doing so.

It was hoped that this program would attack some of the problems that arts programs for children had suffered. It was important that the program discover effective ways to make long-lasting connections for young people with the arts that surround them. In the end both the schools and the arts organizations could then develop a commitment to the arts in education and would be better able to collaborate in carrying out their desires.

It also was the program's intention that the numerous, inventive concepts which evolved could be put to use in other communities by people who wanted enrichment of these kinds for *their* youth. That, too, is the primary purpose of this book.

Why are the Arts Important to Education?

There is a fundamental educational imperative involved in this project. Playmaking, acting out ideas, drawing and sculpting, dancing and making music with instruments — these are natural and even essential means for people to gather and process information. For some children the primary voices for communication and expression lie in the visual, aural or kinesthetic world. Human intelligence is manifest in many modes, and the experiences of school children need to be expansive rather than limited if all of their capacities are to grow. A loss of arts in the schools threatens to reduce the effectiveness of education in general and endangers the future of many young people in particular.

The loss of the arts in the schools also endangers the future of our culture. A generation of students comes forward that knows little of the artistic, literary, or musical environment of the world it lives in, and lacks its own artists to speak for it.

Schools should offer regular instructional program of art, music, drama, and dance to build the skills and knowledge that every child needs. It is the role of professional arts organizations to supplement and encourage that teaching; to offer stimulation, understanding, and awareness of the arts in the world at large; and to provide opportunities for teachers to integrate arts experiences into the curriculum. The arts organizations are the repositories of the culture we have inherited and the structures by which new works come into being. They engage the artists of our time, the professionals with the highest levels of skills and the deepest artistic visions. Just as children are read stories by the great writers, at the same time they are learning the basic skills of writing; so children need to encounter the arts at their highest manifestation at the same time they are learning to express their artistic ideas.

Twelve Michigan arts organizations were funded by the W. K. Kellogg Foundation to explore ways to play that role more effectively. Here is the story of what they did, how and why it worked, and how their experiences can be of benefit to others.

Project Experiences

Part 1

MUSIC THAT MATTERS

... enlightened exposure to emotions, ideas, and varied cultures.

The children who are in today's schools have music all around them. It comes on tapes, disks, and videos; from supermarket speakers, car stereos, TV, VCRs, and boom boxes. Lying among their children's toys are battery powered keyboards that make, record, play back, and even accompany musical sounds with the touch of a button.

When something is "as common as dirt," as the old expression goes, it passes without notice. For children to connect this pervasive environmental sound of music with music made in the old-fashioned "acoustical" way requires some conscious attention. The value of the connection is not immediately apparent to everyone. Adults with music appreciation believe there is a unique human experience in the making of music and in listening to it. Layers of emotion, ideas, shapes and contours, physical sensations, even images and textures, are embodied in the language of music.

The history of acoustical instruments, from the voice and drum to the modern Steinway, is centuries long compared to the 80-year history of the electronic music age. Those whose lives have been deeply touched by that long history and who know the personal value of an expanded, enlightened exposure to such music, wish to share it with each new generation of children. They wish students who know intuitively that music can be had with little or no effort to encounter also the artist whose music comes from a long-term association of practice, study, love, and learning of a heritage of creativity and an extraordinary skill with an instrument. They wish children to see those live human beings singing or playing their music. They wish to entice the children into discoveries of more varied and profound possibilities for music in their own lives. No one could expect to erase the new electronic age by an exclusive return to acoustical instruments; rather the objective is to expand the children's awareness of different music through happy and meaningful live performance experiences.

Regular music education from kindergarten through high school graduation is one of the essential elements in this process. Music is an important means of expression. It is an art, and a discipline. As all of these, it has a natural home in the activities of the intelligence; it has a history and a development and aesthetic expectations; and it has skills and form. This means there are sequential learning processes for music, and children can grow steadily in their musical knowledge through a program of learning experiences. But for them to know where all this leads, for whom all this has had some worthwhile life-long effect, they will need to hear and see, and even speak to some live musicians. This is a special role the professional music organizations can play in the education of children.

For years orchestras have been giving young peoples' concerts. Sometimes these have been done for entire school districts, but in the last decade they are more likely to be for children whose parents choose to buy tickets and bring them to special Saturday matinees. The four organizations, whose project descriptions follow, made a commitment to live music experiences for all children. With help from the W. K. Kellogg program, they determined to discover how to make those experiences as meaningful as possible. Each project revealed some valuable information about how to (or not to) accomplish its particular objective.

THE GRAND RAPIDS SYMPHONY ORCHESTRA

The Grand Rapids Symphony Orchestra, with a long history of giving concerts for busloads of elementary children, was frustrated by the fact that the orchestra listening experience ended with the fifth grade. It wanted to continue the concerts in the later grades, but was also aware that junior high school children have a unique set of prejudices and that any orchestra experience would have to be designed to address the interests of that age group. The first decision was to meet the audience on its home ground. The orchestra decided to take the concerts to the schools.

Schools, of course, have their own responsibilities, procedures, and purposes. If a symphony orchestra is to be a part of the year's activities, it needs to have a clearly stated purpose. To define its goals, the Grand Rapids Symphony Orchestra met with the schools' leaders. Jointly, they decided to:

- bring an international symphonic program to diverse student populations;
- give first-hand exposure to music, musicians, and instruments in classrooms and coaching sessions;
- bring awareness of the importance of symphonic music and symphony orchestras;
- show that composers are a product of and reflect their cultural backgrounds;
- stress that music is an international language; and
- use the intercultural concert program as a stimulus for relating other branches of study to the visit of the symphony.

21

After consulting with junior high school teachers and curriculum directors, the orchestra directors selected a theme: "The Orchestra Brings the World to Your School." They programmed a repertoire with a wide variety of music representing different nations. Materials describing the music, the composers, and the national characteristics they represented were written and distributed to all the schools six weeks in advance of the concert. The programs were selected for their international flavor. During the first year, the orchestra presented:

Overture to Prometheus by Beethoven	from Germany
La Vida Breve: Spanish Dance No. 1 by de Falla	from Spain
The first movement of the *Symphony No. 1 in C Major* by Bizet	from France
The first movement of *Triptyque*, by Akutagawa	from Japan
Danse Nègre, opus 35, No. 4, by Coleridge-Taylor	Sierra Leone/ British
Facade: Suite No. 1, by Walton	from Great Britain
Billy the Kid: Waltz, by Copland	from the U. S.
The Golden Age: Polka, by Shostakovich	from the U.S.S.R.

Each selection was short enough to keep students interested. Each piece was introduced to the students with an anecdote that might help them listen with interest. The entire program lasted just under one hour.

Materials sent to the schools in advance had the junior high audience in mind. They were written so that teachers could duplicate them and give them directly to the students for study. The writers chose interesting features in the lives of the composers, brief plot information for the ballets or operas, descriptions of dances that are found in the music, and memorable quotations from the composers. They attempted to relate the works to the country or origin and the period of composition.

For example, the following piece, which introduces Dmitri Shostakovich, was written and shared with students to interest them in the composer.

"When Mitya was yet a boy his father died. Along with this tragedy, Mitya was often sick himself. Amidst difficult conditions of the Russian Civil War, inflation and famine, Mitya had tuberculosis. Mitya did recover, however, and things began to look up for him. His mother made it possible for him to study at the St. Petersburg Conservatory with two

23

Individual visits by members of the orchestra prepared students for a later performance by the symphony.

well-known musicians. Mitya was a brilliant student, and at the age of 19 he composed his first symphony as a graduation exercise. With this he made a great impression throughout the world. Dmitri Shostakovich continued his popularity as he composed a series of symphonies, operas, piano works, film music, etc. His position as the leading composer of the U.S.S.R. was acknowledged when on his 50th birthday he was awarded the 'The Order of Lenin.' He died in Leningrad at the age of 70 in 1976."

There were also musical analyses for teachers with more sophistication in music literature, and there were quizzes (with answer keys) that teachers could give their students for each listening lesson. They supplied a cassette tape of the whole program (for those who might want to spend only a brief time preparing the students, the tape singled out Aaron Copland's "Waltz"). In the listening quiz, which could be answered as the students heard the music, were such questions as:

The music begins:

    ( ) oom-pah, oom-pah style

    ( ) oom-pah-pah, oom-pah-pah style

Soon another melody sounds in the

    ( ) bassoon

    ( ) trumpet

The next instrument to perform the melody is the

    ( ) violin

    ( ) french horn

Trombones play a melody that begins

    ( ) with repeated tones

    ( ) with descending tones

The ending section

    ( ) grows louder

    ( ) grows softer

Through its creative selection of music, the Grand Rapids Symphony Orchestra demonstrated that music is an international language.

Year 1

Villancico, Movement No. 2 by Rodrigo	from Spain
"One Streak of Dying Light," from *Landscapes, Movement No. 3,* by Chou Wen Chung	from China
Symphony No. 39, Movement No. 4, by Mozart	from Austria
"The Empress and the Pagoda" from the *Mother Goose Suite,* by Ravel	from France

Berceuse and Finale, from *The Firebird Suite*, by Stravinsky	from Russia
Passacaglia, *Peter Grimes*, by Britten	from England
Saul and David, Prelude to Act II, by Nielsen	from Denmark
Variations on "America," by Ives	from the U. S.

Year 2

Slavonic Dance No. 8, OP. 46 by Dvorak	from Czeckoslovakia
Dance of the Buffoons, by Rimsky-Korsakov	from U.S.S.R.
Lemminkainen's Return, by Sibelius	from Finland
Saltarello from *Symphony No. 4*, by Mendelssohn	from Germany
African Suite, by Swande	from Nigeria
"Times Square," from *On the Town*, by Bernstein	from the U. S.
The Little Train, by Villa-Lobos	from Brazil
Three Cornered Hat, by de Falla	from Spain

By introducing a new set of selections to students each year, the orchestra could play for the same audience without repeating any performances. The entire pro-gram could be recycled at the end of three years as students graduated and moved on.

In the third year the symphony decided to provide the teachers with a videotape as an alternative to printed materials. The tape was produced by a woman who had earned credits on Nickelodeon for her children's produc-tion and was working in the local school district teaching video classes. It used the orchestra's new assistant conductor as the "personality" on the tape. The video brought the printed materials to life with listening exercises, biography, and musi-cal analysis.

As the program gained momentum from year to year, and became more and more a regular part of the school calendar, teachers were increasingly likely to use the preparatory audio and video tapes. One student wrote on the evaluation form (collected by the orchestra following its con-certs) that she had heard the Peter Grimes and the Mozart Symphony in class and recognized them in the concert. She liked the Britten least — "morbid," she said — and the "Mother Goose Suite" best. She indicated that in her own preference she liked to listen to rock music first, jazz second, classical third, country and western fourth, folk fifth, and reggae last. Another girl in the same class selected the Mozart Symphony first. She remembered having heard the Mozart, the Ives, the Ravel, and the Britten in class. Another recognized "Greesleves" (sic) from the tape played in the classroom. These student reports document the value of pre-concert class preparation to familiarize students with a repertoire of classical music.

To personalize the concerts even more, the orchestra's management staff set up an individual visit by an orchestra member to every social studies class in the school. This enabled each student to have personal contact with one of the orchestra's members before the concert. Among the orchestra's musicians were a number of men and women born outside the United States. These musicians, several of them quite young, developed presentations for social studies classes that introduced themselves, the country of their birth, their instrument, and the orchestra's repertoire. These visits were informal, and students had many opportunities to ask personal questions and to get to know the performers.

On the day of the concert, the musicians came in style. They wore full formal concert dress and demonstrated their sense of the importance of the event. The con-

ductor, a personable young man, introduced each selection with an anecdote about its country of origin or its composer, and referred to the points discussed by the musicians or mentioned in the preparatory materials. He often singled out the musicians who had visited the school. Students easily recognized persons they had met. The orchestra took advantage of every opportunity to repeat or underscore concepts that would enrich the listening experience.

In this arena, too, the symphony polled students to get reactions to their programming. "The most interesting thing I learned from the musician that came to my classroom is that different bows sound different," said one seventh grader. An eighth grader answered the question about the most interesting thing learned from the musician in the classroom with, "You still need to practice many hours a day, even though you are good, to keep in shape." The most interesting new information for another junior high student was that, "The oboe sets the pitch for the orchestra."

The symphony also asked: "Which piece reminded you most of the country of its composer? Why do you think symphony orchestras are important to your life? and Why do you think it is possible for people from different

These musicians included in their repertoire a wide variety of music representing different nationalities.

A string quartet demonstrates the difference between a violin and a cello.

parts of the world to appreciate music by a person from a different country?" To the last question one thoughtful child responded, "Music is a powerful way to express ways of life." The child said this was the first symphony concert she had ever heard, and after hearing it she would like to go to a concert again. In the comments section was the statement: "This program is educational and I enjoyed it!"

The evaluation process was important to the orchestra as a tool for assessing its program's strengths and weaknesses. A questionnaire acknowledged the opinions of students and teachers and assured them that they were partners in the cultural life of their community. Said one seventh grader in his comments: "I think the program should continue. People have forgotten the value of a symphony."

Deepening the Experience

In Fremont, Michigan, the principal of the junior high school took the symphony experience to new and even more meaningful heights. *He enlisted local musicians and community supporters* to meet with teachers and to discuss the upcoming visit by the symphony. Together they decided to make the "Symphony Day" a special event.

Teachers not only presented the information and tapes that introduced the repertoire but also instructed students on concert etiquette — applauding the conductor, not applauding between movements, identifying the concert master, for example. Programs were printed and students acted as ushers.

The cafeteria prepared a special lunch and community aides arranged to have white table cloths, candles, and napkins on the tables. Students were encouraged to dress up for the concert, and in the period before the event, they could be found elbowing their way to the restroom mirrors, straightening blouses and combing hair.

The students' behavior was impeccable. They easily identified the music as it was played. They applauded with enthusiasm. One child wrote, "We clapped and clapped, but we wanted to do more." The students nodded in recognition as the names of composers and the countries of origin were announced. After the concert they asked symphony members for autographs. In the world of blase' children, over stimulated with canned culture, "The Symphony Brings the World to Your School" recaptured the wonder of the live event for these Fremont young people. They still remember it.

Dear Grand Rapids Symphony,
    Thank you so much for coming in such cold weather to play your beautiful music! That was your first symphony I've ever been to, and I enjoyed it very much!

Thanks again!
Jason Dierking

Dear Member of the Grand Rapids Symphony,

Thank-you for coming to Manistee in the terrible weather. I am really glad you did, because I enjoyed it a lot. If I ever got another chance to go to a Symphony I would really enjoy to go. The music was really beautiful. When our teacher told us we were going I wasn't really excited, but when you started playing my aditude changed.

Yours Truly,
Amanda Anderson

Classroom visits and concerts by the Grand Rapids Symphony allowed children to meet professional musicians firsthand. These letters reflect the students' appreciation.

How to Replicate This

Many orchestras already play school concerts. To enhance such experiences, school leaders and orchestra managers should take the time to work together in advance, paying attention to the school curriculum and choosing materials that complement it.

Both should make a point to engage *all* students. Given their personal backgrounds, it is not unusual for professional orchestra members and leaders to be interested primarily in music students and to think of outreach activities in terms of the bands and orchestras. If band and orchestra teachers initiate the orchestra contacts and make all the arrangements, it is easy for other teachers not to see the benefit for all students. To counteract that, principals, community volunteers, teachers, and orchestra leaders can join to make an event like the coming of a symphony meaningful for the whole school.

It is possible to choose repertoire that makes connections for students to familiar and accessible topics. The international theme is an obvious one, especially for junior high school when world geography and world cultures are being introduced. There is no substitute for conversations with teachers prior to the selection of concert programs. There should be a point of entry for each work — its composer, its style, its subject, its soloists, its country of origin, its history, its melodies — that offers the student a place to begin. Students like to feel knowledgeable. Experiences of recognition are very satisfying to them.

Orchestra people often complain that teachers do not use their advance materials, or do not use them well. Materials should be clear and direct, with pointed information following the agreed-upon theme. Teachers need to be in on the planning and all should agree on a date when materials are to arrive. It is especially helpful if principals are willing to take time in a faculty meeting to discuss the visit of the symphony and to remind the teachers of the preconcert activities they might conduct with their students.

Orchestras should develop activities in advance of the concert that humanize the musicians and gain the personal attention of the students. Individual classroom visits are better for this than large assemblies. A single musician can visit four or five classrooms in a day. Not all musicians are good in this environment. Some are shy. Others do not see the value of finding common ground with the student audience. Some do not have the knack of holding the students' attention. Age is not the difference as much as a willingness to be open, to respond to the curiosity of students, to "talk" rather than "lecture," and to encourage and answer questions. Musicians who are selected for classroom visits should be monitored. If the teachers and students find them interesting, the response will be clear. The same is true if they are boring.

Musicians should prepare to hold students' attention 30-40 minutes. They will need a few personal stories, something to play, some information about music, some information about the instrument they play, and candid replies to the most indelicate of questions.

The "Orchestra Day" in Fremont framed the concert in the school in grand style. A special event that brightens the school and leaves a lasting positive impression backs the investment in the orchestra with a further commitment of class time, staff time, and community energy. Of course, educators can elect to cause as little disruption to the daily schedule as possible when a special event comes to the school. There are good reasons for doing so, but the risk is that the contact will be superficial and easily forgotten.

The best experience comes when it is impossible not to be involved.

THE ANN ARBOR CHAMBER ORCHESTRA

The Ann Arbor Chamber Orchestra is a relatively small organization with a limited staff and a limited budget, but a very high level of artistry and a committed following in the Ann Arbor area. Its goal was to introduce the orchestra's chamber ensembles into all of the 26 elementary schools in the city. The intent was to make young audiences more knowledgeable about the instruments of the orchestra, and eventually to bring them into contact with a wide repertoire of chamber music.

Many orchestras send out small ensembles to schools. Introductory demonstrations, of "this is a violin, this is a viola," are familiar to all. The Ann Arbor Chamber Orchestra wanted to build on these fundamental lessons. Its simple strategy was to create three rounds of visits.

During the first year, on separate occasions, both a string and woodwind quintet went to each school with a program that featured each instrument. The programs were carefully selected to intrigue the children and to illustrate different features of ensemble playing. Experience had taught the ensembles a format that was successful in keeping the children's attention and informing them at the same time.

As soon as the children were seated, the woodwind quintet began the concert with the first movement from a Haydn *Divertimento*, short, bright, and lively. This was followed by opening remarks, introductions of the five musicians, acknowledgements of their sponsors, and then presentations by three of the musicians on the characteristics of his or her instrument. The flute, oboe, and clarinet used music from Prokofiev's *Peter and the Wolf* to characterize their sounds, taking advantage of the associations with the bird, duck, and cat in the story. The musicians described the materials from which the instruments were made, the techniques for blowing air through or over the holes, and the nature of a reed. They asked children questions to elicit their observations. The demonstrations, each short and pointed, were treated lightly — the musicians teased each other and each pretended to have the most important instrument in the quintet because it was the oldest, or the shiniest, or had the most holes.

Then came a performance of *The Harmonica Player* by Guion. The bassoon and french horn players presented their instruments at the end of the piece. The next musical selection introduced the students to more contemporary sounds with *Trois Pieces Bre'ves* by Ibert. The leader made a few closing remarks, thanking the students for their attention; and the program, a neat thirty minutes, ended with *The Cascades Rag* by Scott Joplin. After the concert, students gathered round the musicians for more questions.

The string quintet program was also lively. It opened with the exposition from the first movement of *Eine Kleine Nachtmusik* by Mozart. The violin and viola players introduced their instruments. These introductions were followed by the exhuberant *Hoedown* from Copland's *Rodeo*. The cello and double bass then demonstrated their instruments, and much was made, to the delight of the students, of the increasing size of the instruments — and the difficulty in putting the cello under one's chin. Then the quintet played *I Believe in Magic* (popularized originally by Olivia Newton-John). The thank yous and acknowledgements were followed by *Pizzacato Polka* by Johann Strauss. In each case the ensemble spokesperson told the students a little about the

A flutist from the Ann Arbor Orchestra talks with students at Lakewood Elementary School after a concert by the orchestra's woodwind quartet.

music they were hearing — who had written it, when, and what special style or technique it illustrated. They were careful to keep the introductions short.

In each school there were two separate programs, one for early and one for later elementary children, which varied slightly to accommodate differences in children's interests, sophistication, and attention spans. Thus every school had two visits, one from each ensemble. Because each ensemble had two programs for every school, one devised for grades K-2, and one for grades 3-6, there were actually four concerts per school. Teachers were especially appreciative of the attention given to the needs of the students. In the evaluation forms were some telling comments:

"The presenters spoke at the level of the students."

"They handled questions well."

"The handout materials were very good."

"There was a good selection of music."

"The length of the program was just right for the students."

"Music was shown to be fun and rewarding."

"Personal attention was given to the students' questions."

One teacher reported that when two children had their hands up but were not called upon during a

session, the musicians went over to them after the concert and asked them what they would like to say. Both the teacher and the children were very impressed.

The chamber orchestra provided the teachers and students with a sheet of descriptions and pictures of the instruments with statements about their origins. Teachers reported using these as an effective follow-up activity for the programs. The next year during a second round of visits, the musicians questioned the children about the instruments and let the children describe and explain them. They played more works, developing the repertoire more fully. A popular addition to the string program was their adaptation of Michael Jackson's *Say, Say, Say*. In the third year the orchestra took a mixed chamber ensemble to each school, demonstrating for the students that a chamber orchestra consists of a combination of the string and wind instruments they had previously identified. Again the repertoire was expanded. The chamber orchestra's composer-in-residence composed a work especially for these concerts, and given the year, called it *The Tail of Halley's Comet*.

Teachers' evaluation comments indicated appreciation for the introduction of classical music to their

Through a grant, the woodwind quartet, as well as the string quartet, appeared at several schools in the Ann Arbor area.

students. "This was the first classical music some of my children had ever heard. I expected discipline problems but there were none," said one.

"You exposed children to a quality of music better than anything they have heard before."

Said one grateful teacher, "This was excellent training in manners."

The comment about training in manners is not accidental. From the beginning the orchestra set up its goals to:

- expand the elementary students' understanding of classical music,
- teach students proper concert behavior,
- present live classical music performances in the familiar setting of the school, and
- supplement and complement the music program in the schools.

To achieve their goals, they committed themselves to "using creative approaches that appeal to the age group." It was a high standard against which they measured every aspect of their performance.

Deepening the Experience

During the second year of activity, Ann Arbor schools initiated a policy of asking *business and community organizations to adopt a school.* The hope was to get more adults interested in the schools and to provide more adult contacts for school children. The Northside Elementary School, whose principal had worried about possible behavior problems in the concerts, invited the Ann Arbor Chamber Orchestra to be its adoptive parent. For two years many orchestra members were in and out of the school attending a variety of events, giving lessons and programs, and becoming a familiar element in the children's lives. The behavior question was never raised again.

In the fourth year the orchestra went to some new communities outside Ann Arbor and added another dimension to its program. They asked children to draw pictures for the orchestra; and local banks in each community, which had assisted in funding the performances, displayed the children's pictures in the bank lobbies. The children had an opportunity to express some of their ideas about music and the orchestra made a lasting impression on the entire community. Financial support for the future was also consolidated.

How to Replicate This

Middle- and large-sized cities have orchestras and chamber groups that can perform for children. Most small towns, except for some in the largest western states, are within 60 miles, or an easy day's access, to such a group. Schools can contact such orchestras directly through their management. Conversely, orchestra directors wishing to work with elementary schools can go right to principals, or they can work with curriculum directors, art supervisors, or other administrative leaders in the central office.

To make such performances meaningful in the whole education program, both schools and musicians can borrow from the Ann Arbor experience. Music teachers and elementary teachers can help design elementary programs that are sequentially structured to build knowledge within each performance as well as from performance to performance. In Ann Arbor, music educators met with the ensemble members and made informed, collaborative choices and approaches. By observing teachers and discussing the experience among themselves, the orchestra members were trained to guide the involvement of the students with ques-

tions and demonstrations. The person most comfortable with speaking and handling children took the lead in each group.

It is wise to create separate programs for early and later elementary children to allow the right amount of time and the appropriate repertoire to maintain the attention of each age group.

By establishing contacts through the supervisor of music or the lead music teacher, the concerts can be treated from the start as part of the total academic program. In Ann Arbor the music supervisor contacted the principals, developed their enthusiasm for the project, and set up the basic schedule. In districts without music supervisors, that job would probably go to the district curriculum director or the director of elementary education. In still smaller units it may be the elementary principals who would handle the task. In any case, it is important to work with the persons responsible for curriculum to establish the legitimacy of the project.

The three-year commitment of both parties created a set of positive expectations among the students and remains one of the essential features of replicating this success.

THE DETROIT SYMPHONY ORCHESTRA

When an ensemble of the size and scope of the Detroit Symphony Orchestra moves out of its home in Ford Auditorium, it needs the logistical planning of a space launch. But appearances are deceiving. In spite of its intimidating size, the orchestra has worked to offer a variety of programming in conjunction with its residencies.

When the orchestra is coming to a community, their management staff first provides clinics in marketing and fund raising. Sometimes the conductor gives a seminar in orchestra literature or on the art of conducting. The musicians hold sectional rehearsals with local symphonies, including youth orchestras, and in each setting they offer school concerts. These concert activities can be expanded with performances and master classes of the major small ensembles within the orchestra — the wind quintet, the string quartet, and the brass quintet. With massive coordination and help of local teams of volunteers, visits to Michigan communities, such as a week-long one that the orchestra took to Battle Creek, have been very successful.

To take full advantage of the Detroit Symphony's stay in Battle Creek, a battalion of volunteers was organized by one dedicated community member, a musician, and a Battle Creek Symphony player with tireless energy. Every high school and junior high school had the services of a visiting ensemble. On each of two days, each of the symphony's major groups — the wind quintet, the brass quintet, or the string quartet — gave a one hour program followed by individual clinics for performers on the various instruments.

Because it was not possible to have every group visit every school, it was necessary to consolidate opportunities. To accommodate all interested flute students, for example, players from several schools were bussed together so they could have a group master class with the first chair flutist from the symphony. He led a short practice session in scales and chords. Then, after watching the students for a few minutes as they played, he gave individual critiques on tone quality, posture, fingering, and embouchre (the proper way the mouth is applied to the mouthpiece of an instrument).

It was possible to hear students improve during that one hour session. The clarinet player held a similar session for young clarinetists. His attention was focused on mouthpieces, embouchre, and use of reeds.

The best moments of each workshop were those in which students received individual attention, made startling small discoveries, and corrected their playing. It was easy to see their satisfaction and to see the smiles of recognition on the faces of their classmates as the tone smoothed out or the pitch cleaned up.

At each of its tour sites the Detroit Symphony Orchestra provided a session on becoming a professional musician. High school students had opportunities to ask questions about choosing teachers, getting their first job, moving up in an orchestra, keeping in practice, handling an audition, teaching private lessons, getting an agent, and other rituals in the mysteries of the music business. The message that hard work, persistence, dedication, talent, and ambition pay off did not really surprise the students, although they might have hoped for easier answers.

The logistics of the orchestra's "tour" in Battle Creek might have been frightening to a less dedicated organizer and leader. To handle them she set up a two-page program of objectives and listed under each one the tasks that had to be completed. Musicians had to be assembled and taken in vans and cars to proper locations with exact timing; students from all schools had to arrive in their buses at different sites from throughout the district, also at the proper time. To guarantee participation in the workshops there was a huge publicity campaign directed at teachers and students. Notices were placed in student activity flyers. Ads were purchased in newspapers. All individual music teachers were invited by a personal contact and sent precise dates, times, and instructions for student preparation. The orchestra musicians were given music that the students were prepared to play in advance of the clinics. Teachers had to locate rooms for breakout sessions and equip them with music stands and chairs. Profiles of each visiting musician were prepared and distributed to teachers. Where possible, the project coordinator tried to set up the workshops during times when students were typically in music classes, thus minimizing interference with regular school schedules.

On the second morning of their residency in Battle Creek, the Detroit Symphony gave a back-to-back pair of grand concerts in a huge auditorium where all fifth and sixth graders arrived by bus. On the day preceding the two performances, musicians went to the elementary schools for short instrument demonstrations. They introduced themselves to the children and talked about strings, winds, and brass. To arrange for all this there were more contacts with principals and music teachers. Materials describing the concert repertoire and introducing the music, musicians, and composers to the teachers and children were prepared and sent to schools. The elementary music teachers were the chief targets for this material, and their packet was especially detailed. There were listening lessons, biographies, and style notes. The school concert consisted of an impressive list of classics:

Beethoven's *Symphony No. 5*, First Movement

Bach *Brandenburg Concerto*, No. 3, First Movement

Mozart *Overture* to *The Impresario*

Beethoven *Symphony No. 4*, First Movement

Tschaikovsky *Serenade for Strings*, the Waltz section

Ives *The Unanswered Question*

Deepening the Experience

To make itself more personable during the second year of its elementary school concert tour, the Detroit Symphony teamed up with The Underground Railway Theatre, a mask and mime troup in Detroit. The Railway Theatre troup specializes in large body puppets, fabric and papier-mache' constructions of stuffed fins, tails, and wings that transform the people wearing them into animals or fantasy creatures. As part of the repertoire of its young peoples' concert, the orchestra performed Saint Saens' *Carnival of the Animals*. The theater troup came to the school district a day early, and with the help of elementary school teachers, invited a group of children to perform with them in the concert. The children learned how to wear the puppets and worked with the theater company members selecting movements that fit the various categories of animals illustrated in the music: birds, fish, cats, and elephants. During the concert these children were introduced. They wore their puppet costumes and demonstrated the movement ideas they had selected for the music. Finally they performed along with members of the mime troup as the orchestra played Saint Saens' popular piece.

In addition to the participation of the local children in the theatrical accompaniment to the concert, the orchestra invited high school winners of a piano competition

The Detroit
Symphony's Young
People's Concert
series used audience
participation to help
introduce young
people to classical
music.

Dear Sirs,
    Thankyou for all the troble of binging The Detriot Symphony Orchestra to us. I really liked how the chickins crowed and the lions headdress was neat! Really I liked every bit of it but I can't find the words!

                    Thanks,
                    Leslie
                        Smith

44

Reactions of
elementary students
show enthusiasm
for art in
the schools.

to perform the double piano parts that are in Saint Saens' score. It was very appealing to the children to see students no older than their brothers and sisters performing with a famous symphony orchestra. The whole event created a bond of attachment for the children in the audience.

How to Replicate This

All the elements of the educational program — master classes, ensemble performances, and section coaching — are possible for most orchestras. They are easily negotiated when an orchestra can spend two days or more in a community. But to replicate a residency of a major symphony orchestra as effective as that in Battle Creek takes planning, dedication, time, and cooperation. All of these qualities are available in every community.

The first task is to identify a leader who understands the importance of attending to details. The concert management must have the same level of commitment. During the first year of the Detroit Symphony Orchestra's residencies, materials were late in arriving, and some anticipated promotional items never appeared. This made it difficult for the local committee to live up to their promises to teachers

and it underscored the importance of confirming agreements. It seems timing is essential when the tasks are many. Someone has to round up transportation and drivers, others must handle telephone calls to teachers, others copy and distribute educational materials, and someone needs to coordinate all the musicians' schedules. Publicity for public concerts is, alone, a major responsibility.

While many musicians enjoy these school activities and are very good at them, their first job is to perform with the orchestra. It takes another layer of hands and minds to transfer the talent to the classroom. Where possible, networks of music teachers will be effective tools for coordinating a great deal of activity. Networks of principals and other administrators will also need to be informed and involved. Local symphony guilds should be a good source for volunteers. In the absence of these groups, any local civic organization can work with school personnel to bring about the desired results.

The visit of a major symphony should be the occasion for a global assault on the sensibilities of an entire community. This can be made to happen in a number of ways. For example, by working with an imaginative art

45

teacher, orchestras can devise puppets, fans, banners, streamers, flags, costumes, hats, or other objects for children to use to participate in a musical event. These accessories can accent the rhythms, any programmatic components, the musical themes, or the instrumentation.

It is important not to trivialize the music. Something essential about the rhythm or musical line should drive the invention, and it should not dominate the concert. But engaging the eyes as well as the ears is a helpful aid to young concertgoers.

Connecting with children in the audience creates the excitement of anticipation: at any moment a child might be called upon to go up on stage. That possibility weds the viewer to the event.

MICHIGAN OPERA THEATRE

Imagine an opera company taking over a town. This is the residency strategy of the Michigan Opera Theatre, Detroit's resident opera company that grew from a handful of opera fanatics to a permanent company with two full five-opera seasons in different cities, and an eight- to ten-week annual tour.

At the center of the town takeover is the education director for the Michigan Opera Theatre, who is also a composer and arranger. In one of these several roles, she develops short educational works for the theatre's "Overture to Opera Company." The overture company is made up of rising young professionals, many of them newly out of graduate school or conservatory.

Each of the operas, some of them assemblages of familiar music, some original materials by one of several local composers, centers on a theme. For junior high school students she created a piece called "Music Tells It Like It Is" that let the students know opera singers can sing all kinds of music, and that opera music is something they might like. Another piece, for elementary children, called "I Love You J. S. Bach," chronicles the stormy life of Bach, using his music to tell the story. It was written to celebrate the composer's 300th birthday. Each year there are new works added to the repertoire. They are musically sound, theatrically clever, and designed to fit the length of a school class period. Costumes and scenery are minimal, but bright and colorful;

the scenery easily breaks down to fit into a van for a quick delivery and set up. The productions tour to schools all over Michigan.

One of these overture shows, "Opera Time Machine," takes students through a sampling of opera styles in 45 minutes. It introduces them to Handel's *Julius Caesar*, Mozart's *Magic Flute*, Rossini's *Barber of Seville*, Bizet's *Carmen*, and finally to the twentieth century with *Oklahoma* and *The Telephone*. A demonstration by the performers on the mechanics of each singing style informs the audience while it entertains them.

Two works based on Native American experiences, *Nanabush* and *Ke Nu*, went on tour with the company. As part of this tribute to Native American traditions, the Michigan Opera Theatre commissioned a free-lance writer to prepare a study guide. Besides the expected synopses of the operas' plots, it included a bibliography of Indian history, resource contacts among Michigan's Ojibway tribes, teaching suggestions for investigating crafts, treaties, names of places, and a map of Indian homes. There were historical points of reference from European settlers, references in Indian folklore, and a series of statements about the core value systems of American Indians. There was a statement about oral tradition, and an interview with Veronica Medicine, a Harbor Springs descendent of Chief Pontiac.

All Michigan Opera Theatre study guides are prepared with this same thoroughness, offering an entire curriculum of materials that can be used both before and after an opera theater visit. For *La Boheme* the guide included a table of opera manners and traditions — on clapping, and bowing, for example. Included were the names of the characters and their functions in the story. A biography of Rossini and an essay on the period was supplemented by a table of historical parallels — other events that occurred during the period when the opera was written. There were musical excerpts that could be played or sung. There were puzzles and quizzes — with answer sheets — and a list of recommended recordings.

In a normal season the Michigan Opera Theatre is on the road for approximately 10 weeks. It visits nine locations and plays to more than 27,000 children and young adults. During these visits, the education director gives workshops in composing with all ages of children, including those with little musical training. Students are identified for the workshop by their teachers, usually because they show a strong interest in music, and an interview confirms their participation. They meet with the director several times and all do their own composition, with simple melodies, rhythms, even lyrics, before the workshop is complete.

In addition, members of the company give classroom workshops in opera appreciation. For older students, they also give master classes in singing and performing. They listen to students who have prepared a song for performance; give helpful, supportive critiques; and listen to the performer again. It is amazing how much a person can learn from a guest artist...just because of the presence of a new eye and ear. Often the student makes giant leaps, finally realizing what their own teacher had been saying all along.

In its Detroit home, the company selects high school apprentices to work in all aspects of production, including scenery, lights, and costumes. They come with recommendations of their high school drama and music teachers. They work alongside the professional technicians, and many eventually catch the theater virus and enter the trade.

Deepening the Experience

The higher goal of the Michigan Opera Theatre has been to weave itself throughout a community with such an irresistable feast of delicacies that everyone is left with a taste for opera after the typical week to 10-day residency.

Working through the schools and the local arts council, the theatre points to a closing weekend of performances of a major opera. During the five to six days prior to the performance, community members are auditioned and rehearsed to sing in the opera chorus. This process cements the community to the opera and develops a ready-made audience of friends and neighbors.

Meanwhile, the intern company invades the elementary schools. It gives performances of its young peoples' repertoire to entire school populations. The singers fan out to give classes to every child's room. The classes elaborate on the materials presented in the student show, explore opera terms, and children are introduced to the big opera performance coming at the end of the week.

Portraying wolves
from the American
Indian legend Ke Nu
and the Magic Coals,
members of the
Michigan Opera
Theatre perform at
Christ Community
Church Sanctuary,
Grand Haven,
Michigan.

This student holds a drawing depicting a scene from Hansel and Gretel, an opera performed for his class at Minges Brook Elementary School in Battle Creek, Michigan.

A small group of select children take a week-long composition class. These students explore ways of turning their ideas into actual compositions.

In the high schools the company members work with choruses and voice students. They also make presentations in non-music classrooms. They talk about their developing careers, and the music they are presenting. In addition, they sing selections from the upcoming performances. Company members may perform one of their overture repertoire geared for older students. They may also conduct workshops on costuming, set prop design and construction, improvisation, and careers in the arts.

When the full company arrives for the final performance, the entire community is aware of their presence. The chorus is ready. Performances are sold out, and almost without fail, the company is invited back. The folk opera, *The Tender Land*, Humperdink's familiar *Hansel and Gretel*, and Puccini's *La Boheme*, are three of the works that have been enormously successful in the touring repertoire. For *Hansel and Gretel*, the community's children joined the company in performance. Of course every aunt, neighbor, uncle, and grandmother was in the audience.

How to Replicate This

There are only a few full-scale opera companies with year-round seasons. But there are a number of small opera companies which could put together a week of activities similar to those of the Michigan Opera Theatre. The device of recruiting local singers for the chorus may be a standard operation for many local companies. Experienced local singers can substitute for the intern company with skillful direction. Lecture demonstrations can substitute for original operas for children. Outreach to the schools can build audiences for the performance and teach about opera at the same time. Most of the operas performed by the Overture to Opera Company of the Michigan Opera Theatre are in its library and can be had for a reasonable royalty. Similar compilations of materials could be created by an individual with imagination.

Study guides can be written by persons interested in opera entirely outside the company. A person would need to make himself knowledgeable about the particular work, about the production, and then work with teachers to develop ideas for providing materials that could be given directly to students and others.

Music teachers who have had some of the instruction associated with the Carl Orff method would be good leaders of composition workshops. In the Orff system of instruction students start making their own music at an early age, first using rhythm instruments and the pentatonic scale — or the "black notes" of the piano, because any of the five tones in any combination sound good to the ear. That way students can make good sounding music easily. Gradually, other intervals are added for a full repertoire of tones. Some music teachers feel comfortable with taped "sound" compositions in which any sound, from a banging door to a splashing puddle, can be recorded and combined with others to create a listening piece. When voice — spoken or sung — is added to it, the seeds of opera are sown. Creating music is an important part of appreciating music. Music composition workshops associated with an opera residency and performance can fashion bridges from the student's own musical expression to the finished adult work that is being presented.

It is possible to link the opera with the schools in a way that immerses the whole system, kindergarten through twelfth grade, in learning about opera. Performances of short works, classroom visits, and master classes

provide experiences appropriate to various grade levels. The final performance ties them all together. The key to success is the intensity and thoroughness of the week devoted to opera in the schools.

Many people are surprised to discover how accessible opera is for people. It is a very understandable medium; and, as soon as young people are exposed to this delightful contrivance of singing instead of speaking, they find that it is as natural as childhood.

A REALISTIC LOOK AT COSTS AND FUNDING

An extended visit, or even a single performance, by the Detroit Symphony Orchestra, the Grand Rapids Symphony Orchestra, or any other major symphony orchestra can be an expensive proposition. Costs to communities for such programs can range from $1,500 to $20,000. However, communities generally can obtain funding for all or part of such visits through subsidies from government, foundations, and private donors. Ticket receipts also help defray part of the expenses.

When music programs are for the entire school (not just the music classes) and they provide co-curricular experiences, school districts are sometimes willing to support them in their teaching budget. The cost for an orchestral concert in a school, with prearranged visits by individual musicians, can range widely depending on the amount of support a community provides the orchestra. If several schools band together for a set of concerts, the costs to the orchestra for musicians' time can be reduced.

In any case all such costs are negotiable. However, musicians are working professionals. If they are playing school concerts they are not free to work at other paying jobs, whether it be private teaching, studio performing, or rehearsing the orchestra's repertoire. Therefore, it is not reasonable to expect professional musicians to donate their time. However, you can minimize costs by developing schedules that are efficient. For example, by arranging two or three concerts in a day, at one location, you can reduce travel time. Similarly, classroom visits can be scheduled to take advantage of the musicians' most available hours. The key ingre-

dient in determining actual costs is the "per service" rate of the musicians. That is information contained in the orchestra's contract. Other costs include transportation, printing, mailing, programs, and the usual janitorial and maintenance costs of the performance space. Expenses for visuals, such as those provided by The Underground Railway Theatre, should also be figured into the budget. Simple items — slides or banners — cost as little as $100. Something as elaborate as The Underground Railway Theatre's body puppets cost from $500 to $3,000. Here the cost is measured more in the imagination and enthusiasm of the planners than in dollars.

In addition to the W. K. Kellogg Foundation's support, the Ann Arbor Chamber Orchestra received the help of the Musicians Performance Trust Fund, a service of the American Federation of Musicians administered by each local union. That fund has been created by the Federation to help support public programming within not-for-profit settings where professional musicians are employed. It exists in many communities.

With its imaginative idea of exhibiting children's art relating to the visit of the musicians, the Ann Arbor Chamber Orchestra solicited and received help from a local bank. Local foundations also helped support the orchestra's work so that costs to the Ann Arbor Schools were minimal.

Collaborative community arrangements between arts organizations and the schools are useful in spreading out costs. Occasionally they result in permanent working relationships. For example, in at least one case a long-lasting local arts council was created because of a visit by the Michigan Opera Theatre.

In the world of opera, an intern company is an essential ingredient in the financial planning of a complex opera company. It is very cost efficient for the community as well as the company. Not only does it enable the opera company to introduce opera to young people in a variety of ways, it also provides a company of younger singers for roles during the regular opera season. Internships prepare young performers and identify those who are ready to move into major roles. In one sense interns are ideal for residencies and residencies are ideal for intern companies.

Without the income of the residencies, an intern company would be a luxury difficult to afford for an entire season. Without the intern company in residence, the opera on tour would be difficult to afford in many communities. A week-long opera residency with a major performance could cost from $2,500 to $15,000 depending on the size of the company and the opera presented. (Grand opera is not necessary. Many delightful small operas require no elaborate sets, costumes, or large numbers of professional singers.) Ticket sales would be expected to defray part of the expenses of the week.

Local foundations, businesses, music clubs, student organizations, parent booster groups and other parent support organizations, orchestra guilds, and interested individuals may be willing to sponsor part of any one of the programs described. Most activities will need multiple sponsors. Printed programs can carry paid advertising and acknowledge gifts. By putting together a broad base of support the programs not only succeed financially, but they make a whole range of community people aware of the activity and of the value of engaging young people in live music listening beyond rock concerts.

... expressing the imagination.

Theater comes to us from the most fundamental instincts of human nature. We see ceremonies and rituals in every culture, from the very primitive to the more sophisticated. People dress up in costumes, act out prescribed routines, play parts assigned to them, and by doing so, bring about a change in the nature of things. A couple is married, an elder is buried, a new house is "warmed," a bride-to-be is "showered," and millions of young people are, each spring, graduated into the next rung of society.

The art of drama, which today seems to have moved far from its ceremonial origins, still calls upon that basic need to act out a situation to its conclusion, with all participants, both audience and performers, engaging in a mutual suspension of disbelief. The most skillful actors earn a living by their ability to convince us of the illusion. They carry the child's ability to pretend into adulthood. They mimic; they convince; and, because of their skill, audiences are able to look down roads they might not have travelled and are able to discover possible answers to many questions that begin, "what if."

The capacities to pretend, to create an illusion, to become something other than oneself, and then to elaborate on the possibilities within that proposed new situation constitute the imaginative abilities of drama. In the actor the imagination must be combined with the ability to project that new inner life to an audience. Some of these skills are physical. An actor adjusts his or her face, voice, gestures, posture, to become another person, animal, or mechanical object. Some of the skills require the actress to draw upon her most personal emotional life to reconstruct a moment of feeling or passion. Other times the performer must have a musician's sensitivity to pulse, timing, rhythm, and beat. And often, the actor or actress is most concerned with language, its meaning, its grace, its subtleties and nuances, its structure, and its vocal sounds. All of these abilities can be discovered, trained, and developed in a program of creative dramatics and playmaking that begins in early elementary school and continues through senior high school with readings of poetry, stories, improvised scenes, playwriting, playreading, and performances. Even for those who never become serious performers, drama nurtures the imagination, trains the voice, develops confidence in the body, increases the capacity for story making, and develops a love of language.

Students of all ages, especially those in high school, need to see plays professionally performed, either at their own school or at a theater. Theater is an art form, like literature, music, and art, but students and adults rarely see the professional level in practice. The audience for live professional theater is less than 3 percent of the population. While young people know that their paintings and orchestra performances are amateurish (they have seen or heard what a painting or a concerto is like when it is done by a person who is trained and extremely talented), few students have this perspective on theater. They equate the senior class play with the art form. This phenomenon tends to set a low standard of achievement for theater in general. It limits the imagination of the students and diminishes their interest in understanding the complexities of a very rewarding experience.

Theater is such an all absorbing art form, with its many technical components and its need for special spaces, special equipment, and large groups of people, that there is a tendency for theater groups to become so wrapped up in the details of their own productions that they forget to introduce young people to live theater.

In the Kellogg Foundation-supported theater programs, two theater companies examined the role they could play in introducing young people to live professional theater. Their projects had many features that helped supplement the drama education in Michigan's schools.

THE ATTIC THEATRE

The Attic Theatre, so named because of its one-time location in Detroit's Greek Town, is a regional Equity professional theater company in the center of Motown. It runs a season of productions of new plays, classics, and musicals in a small theater that seats approximately 250 people, drawing its company from the Detroit area and from auditions in New York and Chicago. Attic Theatre worked with the Detroit Public Schools to meet the challenge of bringing several hundred inner-city high school students to what was, for most, a first-time live theater experience.

Student matinees have been a staple of regional professional theaters for many years. To make the performances more easily understood by student audiences, theaters often send out pre-performance materials to teachers. It is also fairly common to have a question and answer period following the performance. A few theaters have strengthened that base by sending a team of performers to schools to give a warm-up performance before the day of the theater visit, to meet with students, and to introduce them to the production with a first-hand encounter. As one part of its outreach program, Attic Theatre in Detroit developed a very successful version of that idea.

Detroit is a huge city and the Detroit Public Schools serve more than 100,000 students. To make the Attic's work meaningful within that context, the theatre's education director met with the city's supervisor of English instruction to identify high schools that might benefit most from the theatre's program. An invitation to participate in a special theatre outreach program was then sent to the appropriate school principals. The invitation came jointly from the school district and the theatre.

The schools selected teachers to identify which classes should attend the play. Each student group was scheduled to come to two different productions within a year. Attic Theatre and the school district agreed that it was important to have some means of comparing one play to another. That decision meant sacrificing simple numbers of students, a tough political position within any school organization, but the teachers and the theatre were convinced that depth was better than breadth for the growth of those who would become seasoned by the repeated attendance.

Each year of the project, the theatre worked with a group of schools, beginning with eight and then expanding to 11, with approximately 140 students each. Typically, the students were juniors or seniors drawn from English or drama classes.

To prepare students for the theatre experience, a team of two actors and the education director prepared pre-performance presentations. These rehearsed and staged presentations were performed in the schools for the students who were about to come to the play. Each of the pre-performance presentations included about 20 minutes of performance with half an hour for students' questions and discussion. A moderator would comment on the play, its basic theme, plot and characters, and present the actors in selected scenes. After each scene students were encouraged to think about the meaning of the interaction of the characters and their dialogue. The actors talked about preparing for roles as certain characters, about the rehearsal process, and about their own response to the play. All of these comments created a base for the students' questions and discussion. The moderator was careful to keep asking questions of the students, to force them to abandon their passive stance toward the experience of seeing live drama.

Artist-in-residence,
James Faulkner,
rehearses with
students from
Detroit's Martin
Luther King, Jr.
Junior High School.

Acting helps
adolescent students
build confidence and
self-esteem.

The theatre's repertoire was chosen from the plays already in the regular season. Steinbeck's *Of Mice and Men*, Alice Childress's *Wedding Band*, a new play by Laurence Carr titled *Kennedy at Colonnus*, *The 1940s Radio Hour*, and *How I Got That Story* were some of the season presentations included in the high school program. As a signal to the large black student population that the theatre is an integral part of the Detroit community, Attic Theatre wisely included black actors in the company that went to the schools.

The theatre set clear objectives for each production. For example, *Of Mice and Men* was shown to the students to help them see the correlation between history and the play, actors and their roles, and the script and a "live" performance. Period pieces, like *Of Mice and Men*, helped integrate social studies with English classes. Steinbeck's play also provided opportunities to compare a novel and a stage script as well as to discuss the themes of longing and loyalty that drive the play. Amlin Gray's *How I Got That Story* led to discussions of the Vietnam war and its impact on American society. Childress's *Wedding Band* raised many issues about the social and personal history of black Americans.

The plays and pre-performance visits operated very smoothly. At the start of the project's second year, the education director of the Attic Theatre did a random survey of students to discover what they had gained from the combination of seeing the play and the pre-performance presentation of *Of Mice and Men*. Fully 85 percent of the students could name the historical time period of the play; 40 percent could name a significant aspect of the Depression; 50 percent could name the author; and 90 percent preferred studying history by watching a play rather than by studying textbooks. They stated such reasons as "it is entertaining," "you get to leave school," "you can watch and follow a story."

The survey also showed that only 10 percent could name the director and only 5 percent could name the actors; most could not distinguish between the actor and the role, nor did they generally have any language for discussing interpretations of roles. This led Attic personnel to consider more attention to the idea of interpretation in future visits. Of the students surveyed, 100 percent wanted to attend future plays. Although only 10 percent indicated they had read the play before seeing the performance, 80 percent recommended reading the script first. When asked what they had learned most from the school visit and the matinee, the largest single response (45 percent of the students), was that plays were done by real people who are as affected by the audience as the audience is by them.

Teachers who responded to questionnaires indicated they felt familiar with the program and felt privileged to be selected to participate. By the second year they were better able to prepare their students because they had seen the value of taking their students to live professional theater productions.

Deepening the Experience

To bring something extra to those students who showed a real interest in theater, Attic Theatre offered a year long pro-seminar to selected students from four high schools in the Detroit district. Again, with the cooperation of the English supervisor and teachers in each school, the theater took 24 highly committed students and spent a year with them, five hours every Saturday for two full semesters. Initially, these sessions were focused on literature and criticism; but when the students rebelled after one semester and asked for more performance activities, the project shifted to the

writing and production of the students' own play. It was the right choice.

The project was guided by a woman with considerable experience as a playwright and director of youth theater. She also had the aid of actors and technicians at the Attic. Saturdays were spent developing a script, providing acting instruction, preparing for performance, discussing the work of others, and putting the final production elements together. Attic staff helped structure and direct the final work. During the year the seminar students attended all the Attic Theatre's regular season productions. They came to know the Attic company and staff, to understand the elements of theater production, and to be confident in their own critical analyses. Students were held to high standards of performance and productivity. They could remain in the program only if they attended regularly and arrived on time.

By the end of the year the pro-seminar students produced powerful work drawn from their own experience. The scripts were so successful that one of them, "Today I Tried," a moving piece about the suicide of a friend, is being considered for publication. The production, which was videotaped by Attic, was shown to the Detroit Board of Education at one of its meetings. Another script, "Crew," was done in a staged reading and incorporated "rapping," music, and dance. "Crew," whose title is a slang expression for gangs, explored the phenomenon of gang membership.

The Attic pro-seminar program did not pretend to be a complete course in acting. Students were made aware that they would need further training if they were to seek careers in theater. But by the conclusion of the first year, Attic Theatre had developed a seminar model.

Pro-Seminar Model

First semester: Develop a script written by the students with the focus on writing and acting, improvisation exercises, structure, play analysis, theater history, and criticism.

Second semester: Focus on the actual production with attention to the performance components — acting, directing, set, sound and lights, and publicity.

When the first year of the pro-seminar had ended, the Attic staff met with teachers, representatives from the Detroit Public Schools, and students for a year-end evaluation session. The session revealed that the objectives of the program had been met. They were to: introduce students to the medium of theater in the setting of peer participation, develop analytical skills for students, and develop and produce a student written play.

The school system recommended that two students be invited back to be paid assistants for the next year's session. This $10 a day job became a fine way to acknowledge outstanding performance and to encourage the development of leadership skills. This suggestion was only one of several that resulted from the exchange of views between the theater and the school system.

Members of the second year pro-seminar were asked to complete an evaluation. Students commented on the play ("Crew") which they had written. Ninety-five percent could identify the "protagonist" and the "antagonist"; and 85 percent were able to pinpoint the climax of the play. In addition, 50 percent stated that the play needed further work in editing and 75 percent felt the play should be fully rehearsed and produced. In a section of personal comments, half of the students remarked that they were impressed with "how far you could go, in only a year, building a play from scratch." These results demonstrate the ability of students to function both critically and creatively in the theater arena, after a year's intensive study.

How to Replicate This

There are plays in the season of any professional company that would make good additions to the education of high school students. Those that have some historical context, those that treat a contemporary theme, those that entertain with clever characters and witty dialogue, and those that bring a classic author to the stage, can all contribute to students' understanding of live theater.

Study guides should either precede or accompany the showing of any such play. The guides should provide information about the play, the author, the setting, the themes, the vocabulary, and the company and actors. Personal contacts with individual teachers also help prepare the school for the coming event. Copies of the script should be in the library of each school.

By establishing contact well in advance of the season, preferably in the spring of the preceding year, the theater and the schools can work out a solid schedule of performances and pre-performance visits. The pre-perfor-

mance visits will have to be written into the contracts of actors, but with some planning they can be managed with minimal additional rehearsal. The moderator should be someone who knows the teachers and students and is thoroughly familiar with the play. This person will orchestrate the presentations so that they are continually turned back on the students for questions and comments. Everyone will need some time to warm up before conversation will flow between the performers and the audience.

A theater with an education director or a playwright in residence, or some combination of these can initiate the seminars for advanced students. Talent in both playwriting and production are required by the director. Students have strong feelings about the events that occur in their lives. They are quite capable of articulating these feelings, but a skillful playwright is needed to identify missing elements and to suggest how pieces can be soundly structured into a unified whole. A playwright can help students shape their commentaries and interactions into honest and efficient dialogue. At Attic, two and sometimes three people were needed on Saturdays to work with the students. Tasks included documenting script changes; scheduling people and facilities for workshops; keeping track of set, props, and costume needs; managing the budget; and aiding with publicity for the actual performances. The adult learners made final decisions about casting and gave strong direction about the construct of the final script. They gave acting lessons, suggested ideas for technical accompaniments for the production, and kept all the students productively occupied at all times.

To get started in playwriting, students need to test out the conditions of live theater. In a good improvisational session the leader first sets up a situation and then introduces elements that can lead to conflict and resolution. The actors are put into those situations to help them understand clearly their character's basic intention and need. The test situations can be drawn from those suggested by the theme of the play or anecdotal material that the students have provided. The written scenes can be strung together in sequence, at first loosely, and then with the necessary connective tissue. Leaders unfamiliar with this process may want to look at Viola Spolin's *Theatre Game File* for a complete set of strategies for stimulating improvisation.

A theater that wants to run a pro-seminar will need help from local schools. To assure a wide variety of students from all backgrounds, students will need to be identified by teachers and encouraged to participate. Together the school system and the theater should seek some form of subsidy to provide a trained leader.

Seeing plays, critiquing and analyzing plays, doing improvisation and scripting, developing performance skills, and creating a production are all critical ingredients of a successful theater education program. Attic's effort to draw many new students to live theater, to give them introductory preparation, to ensure that they repeat the experience, and to offer an intense learning opportunity for those students with a strong interest in theater, can be replicated by any theater company willing to work closely with the schools and dedicate a staff person to an education program.

Chances to see professional theater in action can be arranged with almost any professional company. Student matinees or student special admissions are usually possible. It also is easy to get an actor or director to give lecture-demonstrations in schools. The education director or intern director usually takes on this responsibility. Many theaters have special short productions that tour and are worth considering for this learning program.

BOARSHEAD THEATER

In Lansing, Michigan, the regional Equity company, BoarsHead Theater, elected a multi-faceted approach to bringing theater to the schools.

As part of its regular season, the theater's intern company, which is made up of young professionals coming to theater after completing university theater training, produced two plays for young people. These scripts were selected from writers exploring new ideas in theater and often involved children as actors. One, Laura Cunningham's story of a young mute boy, offered the chance to exploit mime as a performance art. Another, an opera based on St. Exupery's *Little Prince*, presented a boy soprano in the difficult title role. These plays were performed for audiences of elementary school children, and the presence of children in the cast, working as professionals, led to important encounters for the children in the audience, especially in the discussion sessions that followed.

BoarsHead went on to create acting classes for children run by the intern company and the education director. Twelve to 15 kids, ranging in age from 10 to 17, met one evening a week for a variety of acting exercises, particularly those created by Viola Spolin in her *Theatre Games* series. Out of that group two or three children every year landed small roles in BoarsHead productions.

The intern company also developed performances it took out to the schools. These were productions of original scripts, the first two based on the theme "Growing Up in Michigan." The company searched the library for stories from Michigan's past, drawing from letters, diaries, and other primary sources. They used the story theater method, which preserves the literary or colloquial character of the original language. Often the narration passes from one actor to another, and any actor may play a dozen or more roles in one performance.

To arrive at a final production, the company transformed scripts into short set presentations that were grouped for performance. The plays were done in classrooms and for school assemblies, with very limited props and scenery. After each performance actors went into classrooms and helped children talk about what they had seen and heard. They identified the features of a dramatic presentation and developed with the children a vocabulary of dramatic terms.

The Boarshead
Theater uses masks
and transformation
mime to present
classical and original
stories to young
people.

68

Several young people are chosen each year for small roles in Boarshead productions. The company also produces several plays written by students.

Their goals were to help children understand the nature of theater as well as the subject matter of the scripts themselves.

In discussion sessions that followed the productions, children were encouraged to analyze what they had seen. "In what ways did life seem different in the past? How is it the same now?" Since state history is a part of most fourth grade curriculums in Michigan schools, upper elementary teachers were especially appreciative of "Growing Up in Michigan." Study guides provided references for local history reading, explaining the difference between "primary" and "secondary" sources of history. They suggested how children could do their own biographical plays and writings, encouraging them to look at old photographs, discuss family Bibles and artifacts with their parents and grandparents, or study local maps for place names and their origins. The study guide also had a vocabulary list for unusual words that might appear in the script, the "ague," for example, a common expression for a sort of flu that regularly plagued early Michigan settlers, or "Okemos," the name of an important Michigan Indian chief. Also included in the guide were recommendations for other lively activities that teachers might consider in studying Michigan history.

During one season, the company toured a production called "Images, Secrets and Traces of Time," created by children's story writer Max Bush. The piece was comprised of four fairy tales, the first three of which, "Rapunzel," "The White Snake," and "Old Sultan," were closely based on Grimm's versions, and the last, "Petronella," was a modern story. The play was used to entertain and spark discussion of fairy tale cliches with the children.

In "Petronella," the author made the princess the clever and strong character. Students were very sensitive to the reversal of sex roles, and they also commented on the change in language within the modern tale. Like the other works, "Images" was performed with no scenery or props, with the actors miming necessary objects. It was the intention of the company to remind the children that drama is an art of the imagination.

In workshops that followed the performances, the company outlined five things that an actor changes when he or she changes from one character to another. The five things were costume, facial expression, voice, body movement, and gestures. When tested, 20 percent of the children could name all five, using the terminology as presented; 90 percent could list three or more. All were able to demonstrate what the terms meant.

During the same season that the fairy tales were on tour to schools, Max Bush's children's play *Aalmauria: The Voyage of the Dragonfly*, was performed on the main stage. Over 3,000 children gave that production rave reviews. Bush is one of a tiny handful of writers who know good theater and write sensitively for children's audiences. *Aalmauria* deals with the theme of mistrust among friends. It is thought-provoking and full of action. For example, there is a moment in the play when two characters are fighting with swords over the possession of a magical flame. One character asks "Is this what the flame requires?" At one performance a nine year old in the audience spoke out firmly, "The flame requires that they stop fighting." Such is the joy of good live theater for children.

Also in that season the BoarsHead company performed *A Midsummer Night's Dream* as part of its regular offerings. The education director created a piece for the intern company called "Vive La Shakespeare," with short pieces from Shakespeare's plays and introductory material to explain them. "Vive La Shakespeare" went out to schools in

the Lansing area who were then given opportunities to attend matinee performances of Shakespeare's full-length play. With the help of the introduction the students were entertained by *A Midsummer Night's Dream*, almost in spite of themselves. Many were from small towns where live professional theater is an unknown entity.

"This was the first Shakespeare I have seen live," wrote a Stockbridge youth. "It was much better than on a VCR. I hope our school and teacher will let us come again."

"I'm not much into plays but I really got into it. I even did good on the test our teacher gave."

And from Dansville, "I didn't really like to go watch plays but I do now. Our drama and Shakespeare classes liked it so much that a group of us are going back this weekend to see it again."

Deepening the Experience

With the guidance of a creative education director, the intern company took advantage of workshop training given by the national Young Playwrights Festival director, the late Gerald Chapman, to help children write their own scripts. The company first went into a school district in Muskegon County with performances, then the education director went back and gave classroom workshops in the elements of a play, improvisation, and playwriting.

This process helped students understand that plays are made up of characters and dialogue, and that plot must be revealed through actions and speech. In the workshops, the education director set up an improvisational situation in which she introduced some conflicting elements. Students volunteered to improvise the parts. By doing this they "wrote" themselves "dialogue." As students observe their classmates playing out the drama, the workshop leader stopped it at different times to let others replace players in order to have them write new dialogue. She then would ask students to identify the best and most effective dialogue. Sometimes, she would change elements in the action or characters so that the scene could take a new twist.

In a very short time students understood the elements of drama. Each person produced a script on a situation of their own choosing. They read them to each other, critiqued them, and then rewrote them. The process worked for all age groups.

In Muskegon, elementary school teachers followed up the workshop with more playwriting sessions in their classes. Six weeks after these workshops, student-written scripts were sent to the theater and the company rehearsed them. The company went back to the schools and presented the children's plays to them. The children critiqued their own work as well as the company's realization of their ideas. Teachers were so pleased with the intense commitment to writing that the project inspired, they requested repeat visits.

How to Replicate This

There is a great deal of superficial and unimaginative material being put forward as children's theater. Often it consists of quickly devised versions of familiar fairy tales or children's dramas that are merely younger versions of soap opera melodrama. The language is trite, plots are thin, and characters are poorly developed. While it is important to have lively action in a play, weak scripts seem only to consist of "chase and hit" sequences, guaranteed to make children squeal with delight, but unlikely to leave them with much respect for the medium. To counteract that trend, theaters and schools must attempt to deepen the repertoire of plays for young people by looking for substantial themes, drawing on good literature, and casting skilled performers.

Most professional theater companies have educational programming and many have intern companies attached. Such theaters can be tapped to bring good theater to the school. The Theatre Communications Group of New York City has a complete directory of member not-for-profit theaters in the United States. In addition, community theaters frequently have much to offer. The same is true of the theater departments in colleges and universities.

It is the job of the literary manager, director, or persons in schools or libraries trained in children's literature to identify a play or script appropriate for a school-age audience. A responsible theater company should work with the schools to assure that teachers and students are prepared for the play in advance of the performance. Study guides are useful in this respect.

Healthy cooperative relationships between theaters and schools have to be nourished from both ends. Attendance at performances is one of the easiest first steps to

establish. Usually there is someone available, a director or assistant director, to write up study materials or to give advance lectures.

To go through the developmental training process in playwriting requires someone familiar with playwriting and comfortable working with young children. If the education director is not so qualified, a playwright in the company or in a college, or a free-lance person can be effective. Contact the Young Playwrights Festival, either at a local professional theater or in New York, c/o Dramatists Guild.

A playwriting project should begin with students seeing a play. That can be followed by the playwriting workshop. Once the playwriting workshop has taken place, teachers can provide time in school for the children to work on their own scripts, critique them among themselves, and do rewriting to improve them. Following that, the intern company needs about a week to rehearse the students' plays, which are usually quite short.

An afternoon of performances and critique by the students should then follow. Teachers may wish to produce a simple publication of the students' plays, in a booklet to be sent home and kept in the school library.

Teachers looking for other follow-up dramatic activity might try some of the following suggestions from BoarsHead:

THE MOST

Have each student in the class tell a story about something that has happened to him/her that was the most — (exciting, frightening, embarrassing, funny, etc.). One story per child, using one adjective.

1. Where exactly did it happen?
2. Did the place have any effect on what happened?
3. What does the audience now know about the storyteller that they didn't know before?

THE MOST (Part two)

Repeat someone else's "Most" story as closely as possible using the same words, hands, facial expressions, body movements, etc.

MOVEMENT

1. Ask students to pretend that they are a particular type of person or animal and line them up and walk them across the front of the room.

2. While music is playing, ask students to move in a particular manner in speed — slow motion, short and quick, walking pace; running pace; levels — high, middle, low; direction — backward, forward, sideways; isolating movement in one part of the body — hands, shoulders, elbows, knees, feet, etc. Students should be instructed not to touch one another, furniture, or walls.

BUILD A STORY

Let students sit in a circle. Instruct one to start a story. Each child may add one sentence. Help them keep track of details which may be used to bring the story to conclusion.

BUILD A CHARACTER

Instruct the children to choose a real or ficticious person and to describe the person to the class. They must answer questions from other children, such as:

What does this person like to eat?
What does this person like to wear?
Where does this person live?
What does this person do for fun?

All of these activities help develop the children's dramatic imagination. They encourage the child to play out ideas with enough structure to draw together the elements that turn pretending into theater. Combined with seeing plays performed, such activities form the basis of lifelong pleasure in the art of drama.

REALISTIC LOOK AT COSTS AND FUNDING

The principle cost for a theater education program is the salary of the education director. When the program is implemented through interns, their fees also become a factor. Interns in professional theater are paid between $1,500 and $4,500 a year; these token payments are sometimes supplemented by opportunities to do hourly jobs at the theater or to earn fees for outside modeling, TV production, commercials, or other acting work. Interns often supplement the acting company in mainstage productions and sometimes serve as technical crew. Interning is a hard life, but it is the common first job for students finishing a theater

training program. Once a theater education staff is in place, the costs of other elements are relatively easy to project.

A pro-seminar program similar to that run by Attic Theatre, will need a small production budget and some staff assistance. These are minimal costs, averaging under $500.

A substantial production budget is required for any mainstage children's theater production. It should be budgeted into the regular season.

Touring children's theater productions are often best handled with small budgets that keep sets, costumes, and props to a minimum. This means they can play in any school situation with limited time for setup and a variety of spatial configurations.

Individual performances of short plays in classrooms usually cost from $150 to $500.

Because student matinees cost theaters in wages and overhead, schools should expect to cover ticket costs. Theaters usually provide student matinees at much reduced prices, ranging from $2 to $5 per student. Pre-performance visits may be offered with the purchase of a given number of tickets.

A complete play development project with residencies by a company and a workshop presenter might cost from $1,500 to $4,000, depending on the number in the company and the number of schools to be served. Costs would be incurred for the performances, travel and rehearsal time of the intern company, and the fees of the writer/workshop leader.

Local school district funds for enrichment and professional development can usually be supplemented by parent-teacher associations and local community fund raising to bring quality live theater to students. Just as concert artists do master classes or school performances in connection with public concerts, it is possible to arrange for school performances or workshops with actors or writers at a very low cost if these artists are connected to a current production.

Many community foundations and businesses recognize the value of students seeing live drama, and support for children's programming may be relatively easy to get. Grants can range from buying out the house for a particular performance, to the fees of an intern, to underwriting an entire production.

Parents often feel "outside" experiences are worth supporting with personal household money. If a group of children is brought to a program having purchased tickets with their own money, it is advisable for the school and/or the theater to provide a number of free reduced price tickets so that every student can attend.

MUSEUMS TO REMEMBER

... nurturing the sense of wonder.

Every year hundreds of school children are led through art museums, seated in little semicircles at the foot of great varnished images and, in hushed tones, initiated into the mysteries of art. The art museum is the community's access to the history of the world in its visual presence. One of the first known art museums in America was in colonial Philadelphia and its proprietor, Charles Peale, was a collector of everything from paintings to dinosaur bones. That early American museum suggests the spirit of the museum as a repository of wonders.

Today, we specialize in museums of art, museums of natural history or science and industry, and museums of American history. But the sense of wonder is always at the heart of the experience. Parents and teachers take children to museums to show them amazing things, to let them know, even in this artificial way, that the world is made up of many possibilities, and that objects carry with them the lives and spirits of distant people in another time.

It is beyond the museum to teach a generation of children to make art. That is the job of the art program in the schools. But museums can provide today's youth with a direct encounter with art in its finished state, in the company of many other works of art. Museums have the capability to expand children's ideas of what is beautiful, or to enable them to begin to set their own definition of what is art. A child's first museum encounter is frequently through school-arranged tours. Such tours are often led by volunteer docents, community persons who have been trained in the art history of the collection and in the methods for leading visitors to the

museum. Recognizing that a tour's success can be influenced greatly by the docent who leads it, three art museums in Michigan made commitments to educating children to the treasures in their collections through significant improvements on the docent tour process. The three, whose project descriptions follow, represent very different museums in size, shape, purpose, and collections.

BATTLE CREEK ART CENTER

The Battle Creek Art Center is a modest-size museum with a beautifully designed regional gallery that houses touring exhibitions. Because of its limitations in terms of size and staff, the Art Center confined its special three year project to visits by fourth grade children from the area's surrounding school districts. In that way, the Center could concentrate its energies on designing teaching materials and choosing exhibitions with a particular clientele in mind.

At the outset, the Battle Creek Art Center established a tour schedule that provided for two visits a year from each fourth grade class. The Center felt repeat visits

Battle Creek students
contemplate mixed
media constructions
by New York artists
Michael Lucero and
Cheryl Lamelle.

As part of the Masks:
Myths and Fantasia
exhibit, children
studied masks from
other cultures and
created masks of their
own.

would enable the children to experience the pleasure of familiarity with the Art Center and would enable its staff to capitalize on the confidence of repetition to strengthen the children's learning. Each visit lasted about 80 minutes and was divided into two distinct parts. The students received a guided tour of the Center's exhibition and had a chance to create some artwork of their own in a medium and mode suggested directly by the art exhibit.

When students entered the Center for the Native American exhibition, "Spirits of Water, Wind, and Sky," they first sat in a large teepee and watched a slide show about everyday life in various American Indian cultures and how that influenced their artwork. The slide show included works from the exhibition so that the students would recognize and relate the information to specific objects. Because much of the artwork was placed behind glass, the museum staff created special boxes containing the materials used — birch bark, fur, black ash strips, and sweet grass — for the students to touch. In the studio they experimented with sand paintings and paintings on animal skins, two techniques that had appeared in the exhibition. They also learned the significance of symbols used in Native American artworks.

At another exhibition, the "Art of the Circus," the students first saw a short film on the sculptor Alexander Calder's wire circus performers and animals. A printed list of circus vocabulary words was then distributed to help the students understand the terms used in the exhibit labels as they toured the building. In the studio, the children constructed their own wire sculptures of circus animals or performers.

When students came to the Mexican Folkways exhibit, they were given an Aztec calendar to take home with them. (Teachers had earlier received a packet of materials that contained a description of the history of Native Mexican groups, a vocabulary list of names and places, maps of Mexico, important dates in Mexican history, famous names in Mexican history, and several pages of traditional visual motifs from fabrics, pottery, and relief sculpture.) On the back of the Aztec calendar were four images from the show with questions under them. "What is this used for? What is this made of? How is this made? What animal is this? Where does this appear?" At the bottom was a short checklist of additional things the children could hunt for as they walked around the galleries. "Can you find," the list said, "a scorpion, a flowered cat, a glass fish, a chicken with daisies, an armadillo, a tou-can, a goose piñata, a skeleton in a coffin, a musician skele-ton, a candlestick with watermelons, a pig on a bus, a sombrero?" The children checked each off as they discovered them. Some of the questions represented certain themes that appeared in more than one work of art and had been intro-duced during the short slide lecture. Before they left the Art Center, the children made fabric wall hangings, imitating a category of the works in the exhibit.

"The Eye of the Child" exhibition included a great many folk toys from around the world. During this visit, the children constructed their own paper dragon puppets and learned about Chinese shadow puppets, which had been part of the exhibit.

The Art Center established a standard pro-cedure for the 80-minute sessions. As the classes arrived, a staff member would make a brief presentation about the nature of the exhibit. Each class was then divided into two smaller groups so the youngsters could easily gather around objects in the show. While one group worked on its studio project the other looked at the exhibit. Sometimes the children were provided with a checklist game that encouraged them to find and identify features of works in the show. This way they were encouraged to look closely at each object.

Evaluations of the Center's program indi-cated that both students and teachers found the experience to be beneficial. Teachers reported that the children remem-bered the visits and spoke of them often. The children com-mented on their own artwork and also on individual items they had seen in the shows. Some children produced written reports. Others had exhibitions of their own. Students some-times remembered discussions of style or meaning of sym-bols. That was especially true of an Egyptian exhibition that caught the children's fancy. The Mexican exhibit was espe-cially popular with the teachers because the museum pro-vided a lot of follow-up activities. Teachers were the happiest when an exhibition corresponded to a unit in their fourth-grade curriculum. All wished to see the program continue, and there was a universal demand for more time.

Deepening the Experience

By concentrating their attention on fourth-grade classrooms for a three-year period, the Battle Creek Art Museum not only made an impact on the children but it greatly increased the art knowledge of some fourth grade teachers, a benefit which will have long-term advantages. The Art Center visit became a highly anticipated activity of the fourth grade. It was not long before other school districts around Battle Creek asked for visits of their own and the program was expanded to capacity. To deepen the experience, teachers began to develop literature and social studies units around the museum visits. Children often returned to the museum with their parents and were able to explain the exhibitions to them.

How to Replicate This

Clear planning and imagination are the essential ingredients to this approach. The museum director and associates should identify and decide on five to six ideas that can be readily presented and reinforced in a visit of about an hour and a half. Checklists and other games can then be designed to challenge the quick children but not frustrate the slower ones. Items like "Find three works in the exhibition that use the theme of the rising sun," get children looking closely at the artwork. Slide lectures should be kept short with visuals that clearly relate to the works themselves. Materials which provide a variety of activities and approaches to connecting the museum experience to the classroom should be sent to teachers well in advance so they can allot time to use them with their children.

It will not be easy to resist requests to expand the age group if a selective program of this sort gets started. However, if such an arts education program is to be truly effective, it will need to be designed specifically for its audience. Eventually such discipline will have its rewards.

Crafts, if used, need to be directly related to the exhibition and must be able to be completed in the time allotted. It is in this area that many docents are required. Children need help and materials have to be handed out quickly. Activities should allow for individual choice and expression while they accomplish the goals of reinforcing ideas in the exhibition. (Kits or identical copies have no place in an art experience.) People should not expect a highly sophisticated artwork from this experience. It has a limited time for its execution and its purpose is to reinforce the art museum visit. It is probably wise to keep in close touch with art teachers who work with the particular grade level so that manual skills and attention spans are matched with the craft work at the museum.

ARTRAIN

Artrain is the most unusual museum in Michigan, if not in the country. Founded in 1971, the museum was created to take objects from the finest stationary collections and move them by train tour to small communities. The five cars of the train were redesigned to be atmosphere controlled, light controlled, sophisticated galleries. Some of the five cars hold closed glass cases; others were designed to house two dimensional work on walls. The caboose was converted into a studio car where artists demonstrate techniques and speak with visitors.

Artrain has been such a success it has gone on national tours to 28 states. Exhibits have annual themes and are curated by a professional staff. A train dedicated to West Coast Art once featured the new California painters as well as the art of northwest Native Americans. Another theme centered on music and art and included displays of antique instruments and art that used music as subject matter. Another exhibition, part of the Michigan Sesquicentennial of Statehood, focused on Michigan artists. A very recent exhibition, "The Cranbrook Vision: Past and Present," documented the work of Detroit's Cranbrook Art Center's designers, Eliel Saarinen and his son Eero, and that of subsequent artists commissioned by the founder of the world famous art academy to create the school buildings and gallery in Bloomfield Hills.

Artrain usually arrives in a community with a lot of hoopla. Its staff spend about two weeks helping the community organize school visits, volunteer docents, and publicity. Local artists are featured in the studio car. There are receptions and gala openings.

All day long troops of children can be found lined up at the door, although Artrain has never been curated as a children's exhibition. No one wants to be left out. The success of the train was also one of its challenges. How can children have a meaningful experience zipping through the train at 30 minutes a clip? One solution staff had tried was to provide a booklet with a lot of follow-up activities which teach ideas about art. The staff also sent out slides and filmstrips of

Junior high and elementary school students anticipate the Artrain experience as it stops in a small Michigan farming community.

Inside the Artrain, a
volunteer helps
prepare an exhibit.

the exhibition so teachers could use them in their classrooms prior to the visit. They encouraged local volunteer docents to make presentations to students with these slides. A catalogue of the current show was the text for such presentations.

Another solution was to provide a local docent training program. The two-week program led volunteers through the slides and catalogue of objects on the train and made them familiar with the nature of the exhibition. It was impossible in that short time, however, to equip a group of first-time volunteers to be effective tour guides in any uniform sense. The nature of the train, a long exhibit with a narrow aisle winding among cases, did not lend itself to gathering children in a group around an object or set of objects. After many fits and starts, and a few years of less than successful school visits, Artrain assembled an advisory group and put them to work on the problem.

Deepening the Experience

The advisory group was well selected. It included experienced museum staff from Omniplex in Oklahoma City, the Field Museum of Natural History in Chicago, the Children's Museum in Portland, and the Toledo Museum of Art, as well as two very experienced art educators, one expert in elementary teaching and one in high school. Questions for the advisory committee were straightforward: is the activity or material worthwhile, is it grade appropriate, is the vocabulary right, is it logistically feasible, would your kids like it, is there something else we should know? The goal of Artrain at this phase of its history had been laid out: to strengthen the impact of the on-board portion of the program, to gain greater control over the volunteer component, to determine the usefulness and appropriateness of procedures and materials, and to establish more comprehensive evaluation procedures.

The advisory group threw out the old "follow-up" booklet, arguing that it was not Artrain's job to teach art, and that one booklet could not help much anyway. They encouraged the use of advance materials, but they warned that teachers inexperienced in art or just too busy with all their other classroom duties might not take the time to borrow a slide projector, read the preparation materials, or present the slides. It was too much to depend on each teacher uniformly preparing children. It was also unrealistic to expect volunteer docents to be trained in one or two short sessions.

The Detroit Institute of Arts, for example, requires a full year of docent training and docents are probationary until they have completed their second year in the program!

The advisory group then came up with several solutions. The first was a self-guided tour game card that children could use to identify and understand objects in the exhibition. The card required the children to look closely at the works of art and to make connections between them. It established the main duties of the docent as keeping the children moving along and answering questions.

The cards' contents were organized to correlate to the galleries or cars and were specific for different age groups.

For young children there was a page with regular shapes and objects drawn on it:

SHAPES
- Circle each shape that you see.
- Circle things that you find.

TEXTURES
- Circle the textures that you find:
  smooth, cracked, sticky, rough,

hard, wrinkled, soft, bumpy, sharp, wooly, prickly.

For older elementary children:
- Find two things made of the same material and write titles.
- How are they the same? How are they different?
- Find two things with the same shape or pattern.
- Sketch the shape or pattern.
- Find a work that tells a story. Write the title or sketch it.

For third level (secondary students):
- Compare two objects of the same material or medium.
- Comment on whether it is the same or different in color, texture, line, feeling it conveys, other.
- Sketch a pattern or design that you see and like.
- Why did you choose it?
- Why are chairs in an art exhibit? When is a chair a work of art?
- Students were also provided a crossword "wordsearch."

The committee also recommended some systematic evaluation. In an evaluation questionnaire for teachers, 84 percent of them reported using the wordsearch and over 80 percent used the worksheets. Onsite follow-up surveys completed by students showed that children remembered critical details from the exhibition. In past comments the children had remembered only the train.

To make more efficient use of local volunteers, and at the same time to provide a uniform introduction to the show on the train, the staff developed a slide tape lecture for teachers to show to their children. This freed the docent to focus on improving the logistics of the train. On board, the worksheets replaced the individual docent lectures. The whole project made the volunteers' job more doable and more consistent across the tour.

How to Replicate This

A museum on a train is unique, but replicating the train is probably not the point.

To be sure, the creation and maintenance of Artrain is a multimillion dollar adventure. It has all the demands of a full-scale museum — curators, printed materials, mounted exhibitions, insurance, facilities, public relations, and fund raising — plus the added features of moving a train around the countryside and developing the resources of individual communities. Amazingly enough, all this is han-

dled by a small staff that, like its budget, is stretched to the limit. In the latter respect, its story is not unlike that of many art museums.

However, it should be noted that some smaller, similar ventures have sprung from Artrain. Art trucks, art buses, and art vans have been equipped in several communities to take major artworks from museums to schools or to smaller communities. The security and environment is controlled so that objects not otherwise available except in the museum can go on the road. Each one of these has its own logistical challenges.

Probably the most important lesson to learn from Artrain's experience is in the care it demonstrated in defining its role in art education and in its careful analysis of the ways to fulfill that role. Artrain found that "self guiding" is a good device for engaging children with art, especially when time is at a premium. The self-guiding materials were created based on a clearly established set of educational objectives, divided by age group.

Pre-train visit materials were complete in themselves, easy to use, and did not require the teacher or the docent to do any extra preparation. The slide shows, which were comprised of slides and a taped script keyed to the slides, proved to be a good tool. Such shows are easily replicated and can be modified according to budgetary limitations, i.e., slides with an easy-to-read script constitute a less expensive version of the same thing.

One of the most important lessons from this experience is that there is merit in going to experts when a problem needs to be addressed. Although the staff of Artrain was responsible for creating the final materials, they were guided by thoughtful, knowledgeable practitioners in the field, persons who work with children's programming daily and who teach children in the arts. This kind of advice is worth the cost in plane fares and hotels, or telephone calls, or lunches. If an institution does not know the name of an expert, it takes only a phone call to the State Art Council to get started. One person can then recommend another until the roster is representative. Teachers should never be omitted from such planning.

One thing Artrain has done very well from its beginning is to help communities plan for their own Artrain visit. It sends out uniform public relations materials. It helps contact the schools. It organizes committees to bring senior citizens. It contacts performance groups to create festivals

around the visit, helps the local hosts identify artists from the community to work in the studio car, and helps with visit scheduling.

The arrival of the train becomes a rallying point for a series of other local arts activities. In this way the investment in the train is an investment in the cultural life of every community it visits. The cooperative aspect of this process is a model for other institutions that need to multiply the effectiveness of small staffs. They must capitalize on the involvement of local volunteers to make the art visit a special event. With a little imagination any arts organization can think of links it might make to other groups and other events. Wonderful festivals that illuminate the arts for children and adults are born of this kind of creative planning.

DETROIT INSTITUTE OF ARTS

The Detroit Institute of Arts is one of the largest and most widely respected museums in the country. Millions of visitors come to it annually, including thousands of children who visit with their school classes and with their families. The Institute is partially supported by state and city funds and therefore serves a clientele that is both local and far flung. It has a large education department with imaginative leadership, and over the years has devoted a great deal of attention to its outreach programming.

Based on its long experience, the museum set out to solve several problems. In the process, it developed three creative innovations, each one of which could potentially be adopted or adapted by another art museum. Following is a description of each.

1.

To counteract the diminishing numbers of visits from children in Detroit area schools caused by budget tightening that eliminated funds for field trips, the Institute offered a limited number of school bus subsidies. It then tied the subsidies to educational seminars for teachers. To qualify for a subsidy, teachers had to come to the museum for two Saturdays for a detailed orientation program.

The program began with an introduction to the various collections for which guided tours were available. It included a step-by-step explanation of how to apply for buses, how to schedule visits, and what teachers could expect from docents. In addition, each teacher received a packet of slides and postcards that could be used to introduce students to the museum's collections before their visit. And, finally, a focused tour with a curator through one of the galleries, with informative lectures on selected works of art in that collection, was given.

By the end of the second Saturday, the teachers had studied three different collections in the museum. They knew something about materials and techniques, the historical context of individual work, the lives of individual artists, and the composition and aesthetic principles that made certain works especially powerful. "I would like to express my gratitude to you for all that you taught me in the workshops last spring," one teacher wrote. "I have certainly used some of your materials. Watching your presentations gave me many ideas that have helped me to present art to my children."

In the packet for each teacher was a brochure describing each of the collections (ancient, modern, medieval, renaissance, French, American) and the types of tours for which docents are trained. Teachers could then choose the kind of tour that suited their needs. When they arrived at the museum at a specified time they were met by volunteer docents, men and women who prepare themselves to take groups through the museum. As mentioned elsewhere in this book, the museum trains docents for a year before they actually lead guided tours for children. This makes them proficient not only in discussing the works in the collection but also in handling various age groups. One teacher remarked in her evaluation comments: "Since most non-teachers have difficulty holding the attention of young children (hers were second graders), I did not expect the docents to do so well. I was delighted that the tour was so much more successful that I could have predicted." In her note she also thanked the docent for taking one child back to see a particular painting at the end of a tour. There is no substitute for this kind of personal attention.

After two years of offering the bus subsidies in conjunction with the teacher seminars, the museum found the demand was overwhelming. They limited the offer to those schools that could demonstrate no other source of funding, to three teachers in any one school, and to those who had not had free buses the previous year. They also discovered that some teachers came to the seminars without later requesting bus subsidies. Unfortunately, some teachers, even those who had attended both Saturdays, never brought students to the museum at all. Although regrettable, it suggests that the seminars were valuable in themselves for educating the teachers, and the hope is that some of that new knowledge found its way to the classroom. In one year 70 teachers used the free buses (out of 139 applicants). Eventually, the need for the bus subsidy program declined as schools recovered some discretionary funds and saw the value of supporting this activity on their own. Charming testimony comes from the children themselves (from a group of letters sent by the teacher):

To Whom it May Concern

I really enjoyed coming to the museum and seeing the exhibit. It may help me with my final exam for ancient history. We are studying Greece in history class and the exhibit helped me learn more about Greece. Thank you for letting me come and see the museum. (sic)

How to Replicate This

The Detroit Institute of Arts' bus subsidy program was created in response to a specific economic need in the southeast Michigan area. Bus subsidies may be needed if a museum does not have a regular school patronage, or if there is economic hardship in a local school district.

What is creative about the Institute's approach is the way it tied bus subsidies to teacher seminars. With a minimum of cost, most museums could offer similar seminars tied to museum participation for schools. Certainly one of the most effective aspects of these seminars was the time spent by teachers with a professional curator in the actual collection. Here the teachers received quality, first-hand art history instruction in front of the actual works of art.

2.

Eager to entice young people and their families into the classical collection, the Institute took on one of its most engaging projects. It was titled the "Mystery of the Five Fragments."

Working with a toy designer, the curators of the classical collection created an archeologist's suitcase with five realistically replicated fragments — a pottery shard from a Greek urn, the missing hand of a Roman statue, a papyrus fragment associated with an Egyptian mummy, a bit of glazed pottery showing a relief sculpture of a snake dragon from a Babylonian wall, and a fragment of hieroglyphs. The suitcase also contained a manual of clues in comic book style.

To solve the mystery the children must explore the museum, follow clues, examine the artifacts, and study the actual artworks in the museum. When participants have finished their tour and solved all the mysteries, they can identify the fragment and connect it with an actual museum work. In the process of doing so, they discover information about the age, material, and cultural origin of the work of art.

The suitcases are available to be checked out at a desk as patrons come to the museum entrance. They are covered in green canvas with leather buckled straps and stamped with customs stamps to suggest that they have been sent by an archeologist working in the ancient lands of the eastern Mediterranean. The pseudo artifacts are manufactured of a hard plastic, colored to resemble clay and stone. Children can use the kit in small groups. Families can follow the clues together, writing in answers to the questions as they work them out. The comic book guide goes home, thus providing the user with a diary of the journey and a reference book on ancient art.

94

The ARTWARE program uses computers to teach offsite school children about classical works of art.

The comic book manual of clues begins with the story of the archeologist in the Egyptian desert at the precinct of the goddess Mut, in the Karnak Temple in Luxor. The archeologist looks over her discoveries and decides it is getting dangerous to keep the fragile objects with her. "They need a special laboratory," she says. "I must send them to a museum." The telegram that arrives with them at the Detroit Institute of Arts says, "Have found five fragments at different sites. Can you identify them? Ask some other archeologists to help. Hurry." From then on the pages guide the visitors by asking questions and offering charts and checklists, but direct close observation of objects in the classical collection is finally required to solve all the puzzles. Letters back to "Katie," the archeologist, from "Bill," the curator, confirm the students' discoveries.

In order to match the hieroglyph clue with one of the museum's artworks, a tiny seated figure of a scribe in the Egyptian collection, they must decode the hieroglyph with a decoder provided in the kit. When they know they are looking for a "scribe" they must search the cases guided by clues in the book. The papyrus fragment designates the contract for the wrapping and decoration of a mummy. The children must study the mummy in the museum to see if the contract was fulfilled.

All the features of the kit were presented for comment to an advisory group of art educators and the product was tested with families before final versions were prepared. The result is a wonderful adventure for any child, and it is extremely popular with families and teachers with small groups of students.

How to Replicate This

The basic concept of the archeologist suitcase is highly adaptable. Although the Detroit Institute of Arts employed a nationally-known toy designer who had worked for five years in the Pittsburgh Museum of Art's education division, it is not necessary to work at that level of sophistication to achieve similar results. What is necessary is that the designer have a keen understanding of children's interests and a knowledge of art and art museums. Those essential qualities can be found in many communities.

The self-guided tour with clues and puzzles has worked well in many settings and requires only an imaginative curator who understands how children's minds work.

95

It can be as simple as a card or a sheet of paper with puzzles and questions relating to the artwork, which ask children to look for certain features or to match ideas with works of art. It could be based on postcards or other reproductions of works in the museum or of works related to those in the museum. It certainly could include manufactured artifacts — the missing hand of a statue, a pottery shard, rubbings from hieroglyphs, like those in the Institute's kit. These could be made in clay and cast in plastic with vacuform machines instead of the more expensive hard plastic. Many theaters own vacuform machines because they use them to create properties.

The hieroglyph decoder the Institute made was a set of double layered cardboard disks like calorie counters. Holes in the top layer allow the player to match hieroglyphs with meanings or sounds by turning the disks and reading the information that can be seen through the holes. Similar teaching aids are limited only by the imagination of the designers. Museums could create charts of the ages of kings and rulers, explanations of papal insignia or Latin inscriptions that are found on artworks. They might decode artists' signatures by rewriting them in print, or reproduce photographs of details in paintings or sculptures that stu-

dents must study to match with the original. They might match photographs of actual scenes, such as modern day views of the Piazza San Marco in Venice or the Seine River with those depicted in paintings of earlier eras. The possibilities for gamemaking of clues and aids to discovery are vast.

The happy result of such materials is a fulfilling, involved, active group visit to an art museum.

3.

In the third year of its participation in the Kellogg Foundation-sponsored program, the Detroit Institute of Arts embarked on its most far reaching undertaking. A computer programmer who had been a docent for student tours at the Institute worked with the museum education staff to develop a series of computer games that were built around the museum's collection. Because these programs were geared to an audience too far away to come to the museum easily, the game is based on a set of 41 artworks in the collection that have been photographed in full color and are made into postcards. On the backs of these works is information about the piece of art. The computer program uses this information in a series of games that proceed to higher and higher levels of sophistication. The entire set of three games is called ARTWARE and runs on the Apple II series of computers. It is designed to be used by fifth grade through adult students with no previous computer experience.

One of the games, "The Thinker's Guessing Game," is a simple question and answer process that lets the computer try to guess the work of art by the way the player answers "yes" or "no" to a series of questions. If the student answers the questions correctly, the "Thinker" in the computer can guess the work in three or four questions. These go quickly. The random programming of the game allows a student to play it over and over again without duplicating the questions. Here is a sampling of how it works:

THINKER: "Bonjour, I'm the Thinker by Auguste Rodin. Pick out one of the art cards and I will guess which one. Look your card over and read it carefully. You must answer every question correctly so that I can guess your card."

The student selects a card. Questions vary and start at random, but have a predetermined sequence.

THINKER: Well, is it modern art (an object by an American or European artist born after 1875)?

If the card, for example, is Jan van Eyck's "Saint Jerome,"

the answer is "no."

PLAYER: (typing) No.

THINKER: I'm wondering if this is African art?

PLAYER: No.

THINKER: Am I right that this is a painting on canvas or other fabric?

PLAYER: No. (The card identifies the painting as a panel on wood.)

THINKER: I'm wondering if this is a painting on a wooden panel?

PLAYER: Yes.

THINKER: Well, is it Ancient art (an object produced before 300 A.D.)?

PLAYER: No.

THINKER: Is it a landscape (or seascape)?

PLAYER: No.

THINKER: Well, is it something very small (less than 30 cm. or 12" X 12")?

PLAYER: Yes.

THINKER: I think I've got it. I think it's "Saint Jerome in His Study" by Jan van Eyck. Type in the keyword for your work.

Children learn to be amateur archaeologists as they try to solve The Mystery of the Five Fragments, a museum adventure created by the staff of the Detroit Institute of Arts.

PLAYER: (finding the "keyword" on his postcard) Jerome. COMPUTER PLAYS MUSIC AND LIGHTS UP. We did it!

If the student answers incorrectly, the keyword will not match the guess. The computer will then search and identify the incorrect answer(s) in the series. For example:

THINKER: "Saint Jerome in His Study" is NOT something very large. Type R for Restart.

Even if the player chooses the same card, the questions will be different each time. Eventually the player will know each of the 41 works in great detail. Since they have been chosen from among the most extraordinary works in the Detroit collection, this knowledge represents a good start in forming an art historical perspective.

The second computer game is called "The Gallery Game." It takes the player from room to room in the museum as he or she is required to locate works in the correct collections. The screen shows room boundaries and a pair of footsteps that can be moved forward, backward, or sideways to place the person in different rooms of the museum. Children play it in the same way many treasure hunt computer games are played. However, they must learn something about the artworks from the postcards in order to

place them in the proper rooms. Players move through the museum in search of six works selectively assigned by the computer.

The player assumes one of four increasingly difficult roles: visitor, docent, conservator, and curator. The 41 masterworks on the postcards are arranged in 11 galleries according to their culture of origin or function. An additional Special Exhibition gallery is filled with works selected to fit an assigned theme such as "Creatures Great and Small" (animals in art).

As the player enters the museum he or she receives a "Gallery Guide" which can be referred to by typing in a code; it always shows the current position of the player. As the player enters each gallery, a list of clues about narrative content, art elements, historical information, or aesthetic judgment of each work appears. Students must carefully look at the postcards and read the information on the back to correctly identify the works and complete the game.

As the game gets more difficult, the nature of the clues change. For a *visitor* the clues are about the story in the work. For the *docent* the clues are about shapes, lines, or colors. For the *conservator* the clues are about materials and techniques; and, at the *curator* level, the clues are about the work's place in its culture and the history of art.

At the third level, the Gallery Game allows the player to create a special exhibition of his or her choice, justifying it on some premise, such as a common medium, a common period, or a common style.

The third game of ARTWARE is related to the Institute's "Mystery of the Five Fragments" and is intended as much for entertainment as for learning. It is called "Scribe" and it prints out a banner of hieroglyphs for English words and names that are typed in.

The ARTWARE program runs on the Apple II since it is the most common computer in Michigan schools; 65 copies have been placed in all the Regional Education Media Centers in the state. These centers are a network working within county educational centers, established with the aid of the State Department of Education. They serve all the schools in the state with films, tapes, recordings, slides, and other media materials. The Detroit Institute of Arts has a history of working with the centers, having placed their slide packages and filmstrips in these centers to make them available to any teacher just for the asking. Media centers distrib-

ute lists of resources to teachers and promote their use. Other states have similar regional networks for housing media materials. In many locales, libraries have expanded to serve this purpose. It is efficient to use established centers for the placement of the computer games. The games can serve art teachers and humanities teachers and can be provided as educational leisure-time activities for students.

Michigan is a large state, and this game was created to be played by children who have not or cannot come to the museum itself. Still, the game includes a great deal of encouragement to see the actual objects. The game is a natural bridge to a first museum experience or is an excellent follow-up to a visit.

How to Replicate This

It is more probable now than it was when this project began that one might find a computer programmer with art museum experience. The Detroit Institute of Arts was lucky in having a person who had already created some successful mathematics learning software. Still, the project was three years in production, in part because it was the first of its kind. An advisory committee of educators and museum personnel worked with the programmer in the development of the software. The team created the final products, tested them at several stages on groups of children, and saw that they were packaged attractively and marketed to the schools.

Today, the program comes with a handbook of instructions and a huge poster of 100 masterworks in the Detroit Institute of Arts. Now that the Institute's work is done, the model is available to replicate or adapt in any museum which houses a significant permanent collection. This project may well generate many successful, though less ambitious imitations and offspring.

REALISTIC LOOK AT COSTS AND FUNDING

It probably goes without saying that to make school visits to museums effective, the museum needs to have a person to design and manage an education program. The major costs for any such program are in staffing. It is possible that a part-time education director could manage a limited program. But, in most cases, volunteers are needed to augment paid staff. Volunteers should be trained at two levels: to work with children and to be familiar with the art exhibits. Schools run on strict timetables, so someone has to coordinate arrival and departure times to keep everyone on schedule. That, too, can be a responsible volunteer's job.

The major cost to the schools is transportation to and from the museum.

The cost for preparing effective individual tour guiding materials can range from a few dollars to several thousand, depending on who does the work, how elaborate are the materials, and how many are produced. Few places will take on the archeologist's suitcase, but many could adapt the idea with references to their own collections or touring exhibitions.

Costs for extending museum education through computer software should not be underestimated. They are dependent primarily on the availability of programmers interested in the project and of visuals documenting the permanent collection. The latter can come in the form of color reproductions, slides, postcards, and the like. Staff time of museum curators and education staff will have to be devoted to such an enterprise. As sophisticated color graphics are more and more available in computer hardware, the documentation and reproduction of images may eventually be incorporated into the computer programs themselves. Persons interested in expanding on the Detroit Institute of Arts' pioneering work should contact the Institute's education department for a look at the three games.

Museums, like orchestras, usually have a variety of funding sources. Many have local, state, and national government subsidies. Most have individual patrons, and most go to foundations for support of particular activities. Arts and education programming costs are usually borne in the ongoing operating budget of the institution, but money for special projects may have to come from focused contributions. Entrance fees to museums help to support educational programming. Service clubs, sororities, and social clubs are good resources for supporting such activities.

Probably the biggest contribution to educational programming can be measured in the donated time of caring persons who go through the training to become museum docents and who work in those programs. The value of this contribution should not be underestimated. Sometimes these docents will go out to schools to prepare students and

teachers for their visits to the museum. Sometimes they prepare educational materials. Others do record keeping and manage schedules. The tradition of the museum docent is one that keeps alive many art museum experiences for children. The introduction of creative, effective ways to attract youngsters to a museum and hold their interest may also attract other dedicated people to serve as docents. Success often begets success.

GIFTED STUDENTS NURTURED

There are children whose artistic intelligence dominates the way they think. For them music, art, dance, or drama are their primary means for responding to the world around them. Few schools are able to sustain the varied faculty that it takes to provide such talented children with all the resources needed to cultivate their abilities. To serve that population of students, arts schools, public

... cultivating abilities

... stimulating minds.

and private, have been established. Special summer programs, attached to colleges or arts organizations have sprung up. In other places, weekend or evening classes or city-wide magnet schools have been created. Not only is it economically efficient to bring such students together to work with a faculty gathered for a special purpose, it is stimulating for the students to be with others who share their commitment and passions for the arts.

Once such institutions are established they have the potential to serve the general population as well. They represent concentrations of talent and resources in arts education. Many people look to them for leadership.

Not all talented students can or should go to specialized schools. Yet, most of them need some special experiences that support or encourage their interests. Toward this latter goal, two organizations in Michigan, Blue Lake Fine Arts Camp and The Interlochen Center for the Arts, were made a part of the W. K. Kellogg program. They worked on two different aspects of programming for talented young people: accessibility and side-by-side teacher/student activities.

BLUE LAKE FINE ARTS CAMP

The Blue Lake Fine Arts Camp, located near Muskegon on 800 acres in the Manistee National Forest, about 15 miles from Lake Michigan, began two-week summer sessions for junior and senior high school students back in 1966. In the years since, it has become a well staffed training ground for young musicians and artists. For eight weeks every summer, the camp's woods and lakeshore are filled with the sounds of trumpets and clarinets, violins, tubas, singing voices, and the laughter and shouting of enthusiastic, hard-working young people.

The director of the camp had often expressed regret that only a few minority students ever come to Blue Lake in spite of available scholarships and attempts at recruiting. A long-time public school music educator, he was convinced that there was much to be gained by bringing the cultural groups that make up American society together in the making of the art of the future. After all, the arts communicate our hopes, dreams, fears, and wonder. The arts measure our world in sound, light, color, and shape, as well as in motion and stillness, in passion and presence. Our race, our sex, the country of our parents and grandparents have shaped these elements for us and have passed them on for us to ponder. Each generation in the process sees the audience change. In America and in the larger world that audience has the potential to be widespread, large, and varied. It would be a deep and irreparable loss not to reach out with the messages the arts can carry. Blue Lake Camp set out to help correct that deficit.

The first step taken toward enriching the mix of students was to put a minority recruiter on the full-time staff and to send her out to meet with school music teachers and fine arts supervisors in the schools of Flint, Detroit, and Battle Creek where concentrations of minority students go to school. This young black woman had training in music and background as a teacher. With these credentials and her personal understanding, she communicated well the message that minority students would find Blue Lake a supportive learning environment. She outlined programs and procedures for application with teachers and groups of students in each district. She made it clear that Blue Lake had dedicated scholarship monies to those schools. Importantly she talked directly with students interested in the arts and teachers

about the opportunities Blue Lake offered to get extra attention and training.

The barriers were actually deeper than Blue Lake had realized. The camp was not known to most of these students or their parents. It was three and one half hours' drive from Detroit and seemed a world away. Many young people from inner city areas had never left home for an extended period of time. They were reluctant to part from friends or familiar neighborhoods. Parents were naturally suspicious of offers of scholarships from unknown sources, unwilling to entrust their children to strangers, and fearful of what might be a social experiment on their families.

The Supervisor of Arts Curriculum in the Detroit Public Schools was the first to make an institutional commitment to involve its students. Once he perceived that Blue Lake was serious in its offer, he agreed to provide bus transportation for all students wishing to attend Blue Lake. He worked directly with teachers, encouraged them to nominate students for each of the four two-week programs. The staff of the camp went to Detroit and held four days of interviews and auditions. There were 300 candidates the first year; 211 from Detroit actually enrolled.

Once students began to sign up, the arts supervisor and the Blue Lake staff held a Blue Lake Fine Arts Camp "Detroit Night" and invited parents and children to a meeting at a central city vocational center where they saw slides of the camp, met the staff, and heard about the programs in more detail. The Executive Director of the Detroit Urban League and the Executive Deputy Superintendent of the Detroit Public Schools also participated in that meeting. Marcus Belgrave, one of Detroit's fine jazz trumpet players, and a regular guest performer and teacher at Blue Lake, spoke about his experiences there and encouraged the students to expand their musical training by taking advantage of special opportunities to play and study. There was a long question and answer period and informal socializing.

The Blue Lake Night helped reassure parents and students that their decision to accept Blue Lake's offer was supported by people they could trust. This level of involvement with the black community of Detroit occurred only because Blue Lake's president, its camp director, and its minority recruiter went in person to discuss the program with top officials in the school district and made personal calls on the community leaders. With this gradual introduc-

tion, a contingent of new campers arrived at Blue Lake the next summer.

Deepening the Experience

The next task was to be sure that the minority students were thoroughly integrated into the camp program and did not become an isolated enclave. The director of minority recruitment sent each of them a letter prior to their arrival and greeted them personally while they were settling into their cabins. They were paired with other campers, and spread throughout the cabins. A group of six junior high school girls, who had not known each other in their different Detroit schools, met in the Blue Lake choir. They began singing and harmonizing one night and realized they had a natural affinity for making music together. They sang in the camp's "talent night" to wild applause from their fellow campers, and the staff realized they were exceptional. They were given extra training as a group, and received attention in the media. When they went back to Detroit they kept their little group alive, singing together for three more years. Their popular success was a factor in helping Blue Lake draw more Detroit students the following year.

Select musicians
attend the Blue Lake
Fine Arts Camp
through scholarships.

108

After becoming
friends at the Blue
Lake Fine Arts Camp,
these girls formed a
singing group that
later performed in
Tokyo, Japan.

During the summer, five of the students discovered in the minority recruitment program were nominated for outstanding camper awards and four received them. The award carries a scholarship for a second summer.

When camp experience was over, the director of minority recruitment sent each camper a letter with an evaluation form for the students and their parents, and thanked them for being a part of the program. She encouraged them to return. Of the 54 who returned the questionnaire, 49 said they would continue studying the major art form he or she had pursued at Blue Lake. Fifty said yes, they would apply again. One of the most satisfying comments that the camp received was: "His attitudes and manner about his music and school have changed for the better."

According to reports of teachers after the program had been in operation for three years, the two weeks of special attention in classes and performance began to have a profound effect on the commitment students made to studying their instruments. This commitment carried over to their schools when they returned, and it inspired others.

In the initial three years of this program, Blue Lake discovered that the level of expertise at auditions had risen significantly among the Detroit students. The experience led them to more successful recruiting from other cities, and also sparked donations of scholarships from the schools themselves and from community organizations that have expanded the program. In the first year, nine cities were represented. By the sixth year 33 cities were included in the minority recruitment activity. Students in the program have participated in all areas of the camp—orchestra, band, choir, dance, art, jazz, piano, theater, and creative writing.

How to Replicate This

Many if not all arts organizations, other than those that are founded within a minority community, face the problem of being perceived as inaccessible to minority participation. Hiring minority staff with the specific obligation to involve minority young people is an important ingredient in solving the problem. It also is crucial for all staff to make a point to go to leaders and teachers in minority communities to elicit their interest and advice. A volunteer advisory board can help.

When hiring additional staff is financially impossible, it is especially important to have minorities work as volunteers. Specific programs, specific plans, target audiences, and target experiences should be developed. Keys to parent and student involvement and practical solutions to identified problems have to be uncovered.

It is also useful to hold meetings or introductory performances at sites within the minority community. Schools are very willing to work with community arts groups in this way. If the project is attempting to get students active in special training opportunities, then involving the school personnel is critical. Support of minority community leaders is essential as well. The physical presence of minorities is the most effective strategy to attracting students and parents and gaining their confidence.

Continued attention is necessary. For example, greeting people when they appear at programs is helpful, as is following up with letters, calls, requests for evaluation, and suggestions. Minorities need to be on the faculty; there has to be conscious and consistent commitment within the institution to involving minority artists. Years of experience indicate that word of mouth is still the best advertising. But word of mouth has a great deal of difficulty leaping

social barriers. It requires work and commitment to build a positive image.

Blue Lake had something good to offer young people who were interested in the arts. It also recognized that minority students had something to offer the camp. The president and the director of the camp believed firmly that a population of students that reflected the complexity of modern society was a healthy environment for nurturing the arts and for nurturing the students. The camp did not have to lower its standards to attract minorities. As the program grew in scope, the standards for admission, in fact, grew as well; auditions got tougher and tougher. The level of commitment rose with the level of student preparation. Pride in accomplishment was always a part of the program. There was no hint of tokenism or "compliance" programming. Only with the honest belief in mutual benefit can a long-term effort to expand audiences to be multi-racial succeed.

It takes time for such programs to develop and it takes dedication to sustain them. Just because a group comes one year does not mean its members will return the next. Once is not a habit. Special attention may be required for five or six years before the institution becomes legitimate in a community that has not previously participated in its offerings. But this long-term commitment can be built into schedules of tasks. It is as simple as planning, making lists, confirming appointments, making calls, sending letters, checking details, and keeping people informed—the ingredients of good management in any organization. No one should be overlooked. In the schools, for example, that means talking with directors of curriculum, principals, teachers, students, and parents.

Scholarships or reduced ticket prices are no incentive to involvement if the students and their parents have no interest or understanding of the potential advantages of participation in a program. Invitations, orientations, introductions, meetings—in other words face to face contact—remains the critical ingredient required, and one that must be continuous, genuine, and open.

INTERLOCHEN ARTS ACADEMY

Interlochen Arts Academy is an unusual, residential, independent high school located in the woods of northern Michigan and is part of the Interlochen Center for the Arts. Originally famous as a summer music camp that celebrated its 60th summer in 1987, the Center's year-round activity now comprises a four-year Arts Academy, a radio station, and a summer program that serves children and adults in sessions ranging from two to eight weeks. At the Academy talented students work intensely on their art for half of their school day, and often long into the evening and weekend as well. They have the remaining half day for college preparatory classes in the sciences, social studies, English, and languages. Interlochen students, many with a clear plan to become professional artists and performers, come to the Academy from all over the United States and other countries.

The Kellogg program at Interlochen was designed to share the unique resources of Interlochen with students and teachers in other schools. Interlochen named the program's components "Outreach" and "Inreach." As part of the "Outreach" division, performing groups went on tour. For example, one year the student dance company and orchestra took "Sleeping Beauty" on the road. In each community Interlochen invited eight local dance students to perform small roles in the ballet, enabling them to be a part of a professional production.

The Interlochen orchestra, comparable in quality to the very best college orchestras, tours annually. The appearance of high school music students playing with extraordinary skill and dedication gives a boost to music teachers and their local programs. Interlochen's choral groups and smaller instrumental ensembles also tour the state and cities in Michigan's Great Lakes region. For high school students in the audience, the appearance of their peers performing as professionals is an incentive to continue their own training. Students who have previously shown no interest in the arts often are intrigued with the Interlochen performances because they are *so* good and the performers are *so* young.

The faculty for Interlochen are selected from among professional artists, dancers, musicians, and theater performers. They have well-developed careers and reputations and they bring unusual expertise to the task of teaching young people in the arts disciplines. The "Outreach" program sends many of these faculty out to other schools. They perform, give clinics, and offer coaching sessions in the

host schools. The faculty jazz quintet and the string quartet have made tours and done short residencies in high schools around the state. The clarinet teacher and three outstanding clarinet students have performed as a clarinet quartet and have given lecture demonstrations in schools. Art teachers, too, have done residencies. The metalsmith from Interlochen spent a week teaching filigree jewelry-making in a high school in the Detroit area.

The "Inreach" portion of the program takes advantage of the unique appeal of the Interlochen setting. Nestled between two lakes in the northern Michigan woods, the campus has beautifully designed performance halls, well-equipped art studios, and large mirrored dance studios for both modern and ballet classes. The Academy asks groups of students from all over the state to participate on the campus in workshops and residencies with famous professional artists. When nationally known choreographers Nadine Stanton and Bella Lewitsky were in residence in the dance program, high schools from around the state were invited to bring their students for workshops with the companies. On another occasion, Interlochen invited a Detroit high school, which had an active dance program, to bring its students

As part of the
Outreach program,
Interlochen's student
dance company
performed at other
schools. Local dance
students had small
roles broadening their
exposure to
professional
experience.

114

The Inreach program
invites students from
throughout Michigan
to participate in
residencies with
famous professional
artists.

to Interlochen for two days of joint classes, and an improvisation workshop.

On "Percussion Day" marimba virtuoso Gordon Stout and jazz drummer Peter Erskine gave master classes and workshops, and performed with the Interlochen Percussion Ensemble. Approximately 200 band teachers and their percussion students came from all over the state for a steady six hours of programming. At Interlochen's annual "Jazzfest" there is a Big Band Invitational where high school bands from around the state come to play for each other in a five-hour marathon. One morning they heard Sir Roland Hanna give a jazz workshop and in the evening heard him play in concert. Another time trumpeter Maynard Ferguson and his band gave a series of clinics and performed a concert in the evening, each time to an invited audience of high school band students and their teachers. Another event, "Flute Day," so inspired one high school teacher that he wrote back to Interlochen to thank them for the transformation that he had seen in his five flute students who had gone for the master classes and workshops. Interlochen has used this same model to bring students in to work with poets at the Creative Writing Conference and to participate in costume design workshops.

In yet another format, Interlochen teachers have taken guest artists along with their students to public schools in the northern Michigan area.

Deepening the Experience

The most unusual and effective element of the "Inreach" program is Interlochen's practice of giving workshops for teachers and students in which they work side by side, learning techniques of a new medium. The visual arts faculty at Interlochen held three-day sessions for high school art teachers who brought with them one or two outstanding students. The 10 teachers and their students were divided into small groups integrated with Interlochen students, and they elected work areas that were new to them. In one three-day session there were workshops in paper making, figure drawing, etching, computer graphics, and filigree jewelry. This side-by-side learning—students and teachers together—provided the students opportunities to see their teachers as fellow artists, to see them grasp the new process but articulate it in a more sophisticated way. It taught the students a medium they were not likely to encounter in their own schools, and it allowed them to interact with Interlochen students, very much their peers, but committed to art in a particularly intense way. Interlochen students were challenged by this infusion of talent. The works that all produced reflected the higher degree of awareness that the new mix of students created.

Another contribution of the "Inreach-Outreach" program is Interlochen's "Teacher Recognition Day." Teachers in the arts are rarely honored, except by the performances of their students. Interlochen established a way to honor outstanding teachers in the arts from all over the state, and invites them to Interlochen for the recognition. In this way the cross fertilization that is essential to continued renewal of good teaching takes place in an environment conducive to encouraging excellence in the arts. Teachers are rewarded for their hard work by public attention and by association with an institution known for its commitment to high standards of performance and teaching.

How to Replicate This

Any college, university, or arts school with a strong arts program can replicate Interlochen's "Inreach-Outreach" model. The practice of inviting high school teachers and interested students together to learn from guest artists is easy and requires only a few letters and phone calls. Schools can initiate the invitation by calling art, dance, music, or art department heads and asking for such service. The only costs are transportation, lunch, and occasionally, some materials. The key factor is the willingness for everyone to commit the time; students' increased learning should be sufficient reason for making that commitment.

Likewise the practice of sending talented faculty out to do workshops can be replicated easily, given a flexible attitude toward schedules. College student groups can also be effective at performing or showing their work in public schools. There should be ample motivation for colleges, universities, and arts schools to provide these services since they act as an effective recruitment tool for attracting talented young people.

The more elaborate "Jazzfest" takes more logistical expertise: bands have to be invited and scheduled,

As part of the Outreach program, Interlochen's student performing groups tour throughout the Great Lakes area.

guest performers require contracts, and fees must be paid. A good source for locating performers is a college or university which regularly hosts a series of performances. Such events are not uncommon on college campuses and visiting artists often are pleased to be asked to give a master class, a demonstration, or a teaching workshop in conjunction with a concert appearance or the opening of a gallery exhibit. It is not necessary to go far afield to find artists/teachers with something to offer students. Local arts councils can assist in finding persons with solid reputations.

Once such festivities are planned, programs should be printed to publicize the guest artist's appearance. With the current proliferation of computers and laser printers, it is easy to generate these promotional materials at minimal costs.

Schools that are interested in participating in this kind of event should contact the music, art, dance, and theater departments in nearby colleges to see if they would be willing to provide such valuable growing experiences for students. Dance Day, Flute Day, Brass Day, Clarinet Day, Painter's Workshop, Clay Workshop, Strings Festival,—all such activities are possible with only a little planning and

coordination. Participation in such a workshop can be a way of rewarding students who show serious commitment to their art. It can also spark some serious learning in talented students who have not yet decided their career path.

For those who have not conducted such a program, there are a few basic formats to follow. A typical instrumental *music* workshop might consist of the master teacher demonstrating performance techniques and playing a few works that illustrate those techniques. These could be fingering patterns, bowing patterns, embouchre exercises, mallet or stick techniques, approaches to understanding dynamics, approaches to playing certain composers' music; rehearsal strategies or practice strategies. Students are usually asked to bring instruments and to try techniques demonstrated. The master teacher critiques individuals or the group. Some teachers concentrate on demonstrations and performing; others concentrate on critiques of students' performances. A long session, of more than a half day, should feature some of both.

It is especially gratifying for student groups to perform for each other. They take great pride in sharing their accomplishments. Performances that are accompanied by brief explanations of pieces in the repertoire—why they were chosen, what they represent historically and stylistically, which students will perform solos, which parts are exceptionally difficult, who is the composer—add to everyone's musical knowledge.

A workshop in an *art* area requires each student to have access to materials and equipment. In a weaving studio there would have to be enough looms to accommodate the group; in a clay studio one expects enough wheels for throwing, or tables for other construction techniques. The number of students needs to be limited to the size of the studio. A visual arts workshop might offer several techniques so that a group of 40 to 50 could participate by dividing the group according to interest. It would be wise to allow more than one session for students to finish a work in a visual arts medium. However, opportunities to hear and see artists who are just passing through also have their rewards.

The chapters of Music Educators National Conference, to which most music teachers belong, (elementary and secondary schools and colleges included) is a natural communications network for bringing music students and teachers together for special workshops. The American String Teachers Association is another. Chapters of the National Art Education Association exist in every state and link college teachers with those in K-12 education. State chapters of the National Dance Association and state theater associations do the same for their disciplines. The members of these associations can usually identify outstanding performers and teachers who would offer the kind of master classes or clinics that students profit from the most. Arts academies and schools hoping to bind young artists to them and to the future of the discipline will want to consider that prospect.

All of these professional associations have annual conferences and showcases. The Interlochen outreach and inreach is a model that goes beyond the showcase to the intimacy of the studio and classroom.

The concept of side-by-side learning requires only the willingness of teachers to agree to the process. Experienced artists and performers can be brought into a classroom over a period of a few days to give classes for students and teachers. Colleges, art schools, music academies, and conservatories are sources of master teachers. Independent artists also are willing to engage in residencies. State and local arts councils have lists of people with experience. A

The faculty for Interlochen is chosen from among professional artists, dancers, musicians, and theater performers.

group of teachers in a district, or a group of teachers across a few small districts could stage such an experience. Projects can be structured to involve only highly interested students or all students in a class. The side-by-side learning projects are most effective when there are several sessions, each allotting enough time to complete a project and to get to know one another.

A REALISTIC LOOK AT COSTS AND FUNDING

In creating minority opportunities, such as Blue Lake did, the main cost is staff time. Sufficient staff time must be devoted to changing the perception that the programs are really not meant for anyone but those already in them. If you wish to change the course of a river, you have to dig a very deep trench, and even then the waters will resist the slightest obstacle and hide in the shallowest depressions. Committing staff time and staff attitude is the key to making a change in audience behavior.

Where scholarships or reduced ticket prices or transportation is necessary, a host of local agencies stand ready to assist young people to improve their opportunities. Community foundations, community service groups, sororities, fraternities, parent groups, church groups, and the schools are generally all willing to help.

The costs to replicate many of Interlochen's outreach-inreach programs are minimal. Fees to guest artists, and the cost of their transportation and lodging, are the only significant considerations. When a professional performer comes to town to do a concert, the largest expense is supported by ticket admissions. It makes sense to combine those performance appearances with classes for students and teachers. When a visual artist has an exhibition, he or she is often present for the opening. That is a prime time to hold a master class.

In many art schools or conservatories, colleges or universities, the artists may offer the outreach experience as part of their normal faculty obligations. In that case, transportation and housing of students are a consideration if the project is overnight at a distant location. Vans and private cars can minimize those expenses. Colleges can sometimes house guest students in dormitories for a nominal amount.

DANCE GETS AROUND

... nurturing the power to focus energy and attention.

Anthropologists and zoologists confirm that dance is a phenomenon that crosses the barriers of species and cultures. Bipeds, both furred and feathered, quadripeds, possibly even fish, dance. They make rhythmic and repeated movements that have some celebratory or ritualistic function. Dances are sometimes ceremonial. Many creatures, including humans, dance as a ritual of courtship. Some dances are solitary, some are communal—for pleasure, as magic, to mourn and to cheer, to lament and to encourage.

Dance can take exotic forms. In classical ballet, dancers stretch and strengthen their bodies beyond normal capacities so that they can form artful and elegant shapes while, with the help of a padded slipper, the foot is made to carry the entire weight of the body on the point of a toe. Elsewhere, as in Bali, dancers have their hip joints rolled with poles to effect a complete 180 degree turnout of the legs.

But even with this extreme exertion of physical ability on the one hand, there remains, on the other, the dance that is a simple and natural response to music, to rhythm, and to the imagination. At all levels, dance is a means of communication of emotion, images, and ideas. For some people it is a primary means of expression, carrying in it the power to focus energy and attention, to clarify thought, to speak through space, time, force, and shape.

Dance is a natural component of education, nurturing the coordination of the large and small motor skills, linking ideas through movement, and providing an avenue for emotional expression that leaves the student "at home" in his or her body. Dance is easily linked to a program in music education and to physical education. It has its logical ties to art education, where children are learning about shapes, space, and composition, and it is connected to drama through its capacity to engage children in imagining themselves as other people, animals, machines, or objects in nature. A dance specialist in the schools can help children receive a steadily progressing diet of dance education throughout their schooling. Eventually, dance education leads to children finding the aspect of dance that will go with them into the adult world. A few will become professional dancers, more will become social dancers, and others will become the audience for dance.

In spite of what might seem to be a reasonable case for dance in the schools, very few dance education programs exist in American K-12 systems. It is rare for schools to have any systematic teaching in dance. Where it exists it is usually limited to learning a few folk, square, and round dances. Dance has been anathema to boys, and only a small number of physical education persons are sufficiently trained in dance to offer a comprehensive program.

Dance is generally the Cinderella of the arts, but with no fairy godmother to help her out. Dancers and dance companies all over the country have tried to change this situation and give dance an opportunity to demonstrate its capacities to educate. In Michigan, dance was assisted by a statewide organizational effort.

THE MICHIGAN DANCE ASSOCIATION

The Michigan Dance Association is a service organization designed to raise the status of dance through a variety of means. A long-term goal has been to improve dance education in the elementary and secondary schools. Members include private dance teachers, independent dancers and choreographers, university and public schools dance teachers, and dance enthusiasts.

Borrowing an idea from a successful but very expensive National Endowment for the Arts program called Dancers-in-the-Schools, the Michigan Dance Association created a Michigan Dancers-in-Schools project. The project fostered extended residencies with dance specialists who gave a series of workshops for teachers, and a series of classes for students. It also included performances by dance companies. Numbered among the dance specialists were several university dance faculty members, the director of a resident professional dance company in Lansing, the director of the Midland Young Peoples' Dance Troup at the Midland Community Center, the director of a Flamenco Dance Troup in Detroit, the director of a group called ProMotion that is based at Northern Michigan University and specializes in movement games for perpetual enhancement, and a dance therapist who is the founder of the Dance Kaleidoscope Company of Indianapolis. To become a specialist in the program one had to audition for a group of experts in dance for children, as did the dance companies. Both the specialists and the companies were varied, including university dance companies, a children's dance troup, and three professional companies whose repertory is in the modern arena.

The dance specialists introduced principles of dance to teachers and involved children of different age levels in exploring dance ideas. Since dance is very much undeveloped in most schools, these classes were usually on the beginning level. Most of the residencies were at elementary

Dance helps children
link ideas through
movement, and
nurtures the
coordination of large
and small motor
skills.

schools in a district. Following the weeks of dance classes, a dance company would come in to give a lecture demonstration, with finished dance works and explanations of the techniques and choreographic ideas. Sometimes a full-scale public concert was included in the residency.

In one year the Michigan Dance Association program engaged the services of 15 dance consultants and four companies, all of whom had auditioned to be part of the project. A total of 12,700 students and 413 teachers were involved in 62 schools.

Meetings establishing the entire residency were held at each project site. Principals, teachers, and usually, the director of physical education, met with the Michigan Dance Association personnel. When a residency began, the dance consultant provided a session for staff orientation in which the basic assumptions and goals of the program were explained and teachers were introduced to the concepts that would be taught to the students. This was followed by workshops with the students in the gym or studio, one class at a time. The consultant introduced dance and creative movement exercises that revealed the standard dance vocabulary. Each group of students had at least two such workshops.

In these classes students learned the difference between sustained, percussive, locomotor, and vibratory movement. They learned to recognize the elements of force, time, level, and movement quality that exist in everyday life and that can be organized and transformed into dance. The consultant also reinforced academic concepts—one class explored the idea of symmetry and asymmetry, another worked on the concepts of similarity and contrast, while another confronted number patterns, or basic shapes, or the more subtle language of harmony and dissonance. The consultant spent time with individual teachers before taking the class into the dance workshop. In this way the two teachers reinforced each others' purposes. The residency closed with a lecture demonstration or performance with a dance company. Before the consultant finished there was at least one more session with teachers, providing follow-up materials and ideas for extending the concepts taught in the dance classes.

Two goals guided all activities:

1. Create an opportunity for every child to experience dance as an art form within the school curriculum.
2. Provide teachers with methods to explore creative dance activities with their students. The basic assumptions are

The Michigan Dance
Association program
gave children of all
ages and abilities the
chance to experience
dance as an art form.

that dance is an inherently valuable activity and that exposure to dance, as children, will foster adult participation.

Likewise each class was expected to: introduce children to dance and creative movement, reveal the vocabulary of dance, and reinforce academic concepts through dance.

Exercises to accomplish all of these dance classes explored space, time, and force in dance. They introduced a guiding concept for each session such as rhythm and pattern, travel in time, levels of space, positive and negative shape. Students could learn to map floor patterns, to create movements on different levels, to work in mirror images, to repeat movements created by others, to analyze movement in terms of means of support, and to vary movement character from sustained to percussive to vibratory to locomotor. They could connect dance to characteristics of movement in machines, in animals, in wind or water. They could take movement ideas from sounds, words, pictures, or music. They could try to create a short sequence of movement and memorize it and perform it for the rest of the class. They might analyze and practice basic locomotor movements like running, hopping, skipping and leaping, and try out dance falls or turns. All of these activities were adjusted to age levels and to ideas that teachers found compatible with work they were doing in other classes. Students studying the planets, for example, might work on a dance that explores concentric circles and turning within circles. Students studying multiplication could explore rhythmic movement patterns of multiples of threes.

The essence of this work was that dance is an art encompassing the body in space. The project promoted the idea that children and adults should begin their study of dance from a broad perspective, then gradually develop the physical techniques of strong and flexible limbs, good balance, and a precise sense of direction through further training. These sessions were such a beginning.

Deepening the Experience

Because dance is so seldom taught in regular teacher preparation and there are few dance specialists in schools in general, the Michigan Dancers-in-Schools program always involved a teacher inservice education session. Teachers were presented with the techniques and purposes of

Always popular with children, the "Bag-it" routine is performed here by a member of the Detroit Dance Collective.

I liked the part where they were in the bags.

"Bag-it" was the hands-down favorite of this young dance fan.

the dance program. They were given a few simple strategies for expanding the dance ideas in their own classrooms. They were encouraged to take the dance class along with their students. Again, the dance specialists studied the elementary curriculum and made explicit connections between dance and other concepts that teachers were concerned with. In one school, in the same year they studied the Spanish influence on Mexican culture, the sixth grade teachers worked with a Flamenco style Spanish dancer. For obvious reasons, the teachers and children were very responsive to the dance component in that program.

Many schools repeated the program for as many as three years, with different specialists and dance companies, and with increasing levels of competence in their students and teachers. In the second year the number of workshops with students increased. Seeing various dance companies means that the students have a chance to identify different types of dance and different approaches to choreography.

In Berkeley, Michigan, a comment by a physical education facilitator for the schools revealed the climate for the Michigan Dancers-in-Schools project.

I think we were all a little skeptical of this program at first because we knew so little about it. Now that we have experienced it, we are no longer skeptical. I can honestly say it is a popular consensus that we try to keep this program as a permanent part of our elementary physical education curriculum. From my standpoint as the elementary P.E. facilitator, the Michigan Dancers-in-Schools program reinforces our movement program and introduces new ideas and ways to implement it. I wish you could have watched the creative movements the specialist's lessons stimulated our students to do.

One more teacher expressed the same thoughts as her colleague above:

Inasmuch as I felt that my students would find it difficult to get into the mood, it turned out to be just the opposite. They enjoyed the program and became quite involved in what they were doing. It was even good therapy for some of the little boys that still have not developed fine motor control. The class encouraged the students to express themselves through rhythmic movement—such as joy, anger, or to learn lessons visually from science, math, etc.

Another principal echoed his assessment by stating that:

I think it will take several more exposures (years) before we will have teachers automatically including these techniques in their 'bag of tricks.' Nevertheless, these two years have built awareness and willingness to try new ideas. Many seem convinced of the validity of movement education in our teaching program, so I can see real growth.

At Winans Elementary School in Lansing the arts specialist wrote:

I have seen growth in our staff as a result of the program. More and more teachers sign up to participate each year because they are recognizing the relevance of Movement Education in our curriculum. They are willing to spend time using this medium because it enhances and enriches that which they already teach.

In several school districts, the Dancers-in-Schools program led to a district-wide commitment to a dance program as part of the regular curriculum. This, of course, is the ultimate goal of the Michigan Dancers-in-Schools project.

As the Michigan Dancers-in-Schools program grew, it took on another important component: dance for handicapped children and adults. Several dance therapists have long been members of the Michigan Dance Association. Through the network of the Very Special Arts Festivals, a national program located at the Kennedy Center in Washington which has a number of state affiliates, these specialists began to create an awareness of the capacity for dance that all children possess, including those with physical and mental impairments. Even before the residencies on the Michigan model, dance therapists went into the special schools and centers where handicapped youngsters are educated. Gradually, using the Dancers-in-Schools structure, they provided workshops for teachers and caregivers in movement, and they worked directly with the children.

Dance therapists selected movements which drew handicapped people into full participation— simple bends, reaching out, stepping side to side, or exploring space with an object like a ball or a scarf. Through the effort, some students found an unusual outlet for emotional expression; others sensed a liberating opportunity for physical movement. In a few cases, the dance project successfully integrated the handicapped students with the regular classroom students. All benefited from the program.

How to Replicate This

Care should be taken that the first dance experiences of young children, particularly those in preschool, first and second grade, are broadly based in rhythmic responses to music and creative movement. The specific techniques of ballet, tap, modern dance, ethnic dance, and folk dances, are most effective when children have the experience and muscle coordination to execute and enjoy the forms. Such coordination begins to occur at about age seven or eight. Before that, children can be engaged in skipping, hopping, level changing, making shapes, marching, handclapping, stretching, contracting, balancing, bending, rising and falling, and responding with movement to many stimuli—music, rhythmic instruments, animal shapes, environmental sounds, traffic noises, floor patterns, sculpture and painted shapes, and movements of the body. Gradually children take an interest in formalizing movements, learning the vocabulary of traditional dances, and creating their own complete memorized compositions. The goal should be to engage the students in an understanding of dance within their own bodies and within the art form as a whole.

The statewide network for a particular art form, especially dance and theater, is practical. Travel costs are contained by sending people to serve several projects within a particular area. Sometimes the Dance Association can find a specialist or a company that is located near the school requesting service. Standards for program quality and for qualified individuals can be established through a professional clearinghouse. The administrative work of scheduling and fund raising can be handled by a single office, relieving small arts organizations of the burden, and providing the public with a readily accessible person—one who understands schools, school schedules, curriculum and teacher needs, as well as the needs and the nature of the art form. Evaluation can be conducted on a scale that gives meaningful results.

This structure is especially important for dance because few companies are so substantially fixed that they have the administrative support for touring and educational programming. Many small companies rehearse in spare time for other jobs and gather in a director's private studio. Some are attached in an ad hoc fashion to colleges and universities. Others have short seasons and disperse for remaining months. Dance specialists with training and interest in children's dance and dance in the schools may be isolated from one another because they are free-lance artists, teach in their own private studio, or work in a one-person college department. A regional association can provide an important central information source both for dancers and for schools.

With or without the central structure, small dance companies that have people experienced in dance education can provide an effective residency. Whatever the source, the residency should include sessions with teachers, repeated sessions with classes of students, and performance by professionals. Only then may students and teachers form a definite idea of what the finished product of concert dance looks like.

For names of dancers and dance companies, consult your state or local arts council or your local college's dance department. Ask for dancers trained and interested in dance for children. For years the Dance Department at Wayne State University has been training faculty in children's dance. Its pioneer educator, Ruth Murray, has written some of the leading work in the field. It is still a good reference for determining the critical elements of a dance program for children.

A REALISTIC LOOK AT COSTS AND FUNDING

Probably the most creative aspect of the Michigan Dancers-in-Schools project was its ability to develop funding sources for residencies. The state arts council funded a number of the residencies in their Arts-in-Education program. The Dance Association assisted local school districts in writing proposals, a process which helped prepare the school administration for the residency and ensured that the district got the full range of services. The Very Special Arts program helped support dance for handicapped students. Local sponsors also contributed to the dance projects.

Districts were required to fund part of the residency themselves. Because the residencies were structured comprehensively and affected large numbers of students, the schools felt the project was worth the expense.

The residency of a dance specialist can be negotiated with the individual. The important element is to establish a presence of dance for a period of time. The specialist should be able to give repeated sessions, should be willing to work with teachers, and, therefore, should represent the cost of buying an artist's time for three to four hours a day for two to three weeks.

As with any artist or educational program, it would be wise to preview a dance company before bringing it in to perform. Any responsible company will provide video-tapes of its work or will refer a prospective host to places where the company has performed. State arts councils have lists of groups they have critiqued. Arts Midwest, a regional organization in Minneapolis, has a list of recommended performance organizations. Sometimes there are programs that offer subsidies for the fees of dance companies; such sub-sidies are often offered by state arts councils as incentives for people to present dance.

Ticket sales will help defray the cost of a performance, but they will probably not pay for the entire cost of bringing in a professional company.

Basic lessons in dance are an inexpensive way to introduce children to fine arts.

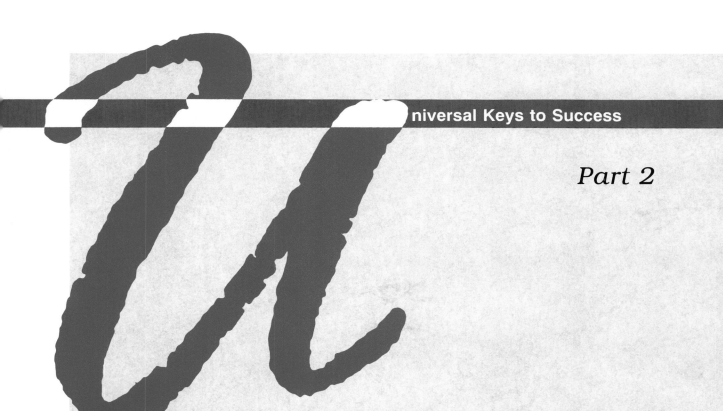

Part 2

... setting ground rules for the event.

This is not a book of rules or recipes. Each project had its own unique experiences, its own special ingredients. However, certain common elements were present in all cases. They are collected here to focus on their specific importance to any program you may undertake.

1. Plan in Common

As commonplace as it sounds, there is no substitute for planning. When a school takes on an arts project involving external resources, and when an arts organization takes on work in schools, both are adding responsibilities to already busy people. It will be tempting, but foolhardy, to minimize the amount of time needed to plan an arts event.

The first step to a mutually satisfying educational artistic experience is to involve both the arts organization and the schools in the planning from the beginning. If the project is going to work, it needs to be something everyone wants to do. Ask what are we doing? Why are we doing this? What do we want to get out of it? The more people know what each other expects, the easier it will be to satisfy their wants and needs.

Says Poor Richard: "A little neglect breeds great mischief. For want of a nail the shoe was lost, for want of a shoe a horse was lost, for want of a horse the rider was lost, for want of a rider the battle was lost, and all for the want of a horseshoe nail." In the end everything is a matter of details. Where should people park? What door do they come in? What equipment is needed and in what room at what time? How many students will be involved? What ages? What are the names of all the teachers and artists? Who will do the intro-

ductions? Exactly how much time will we have? Will the supplies be there when the artists arrive? What will the students need to know? Who will tell them? Will the participating teachers handle discipline problems? Who will make contacts for the buses? When will tickets be delivered? On what date do we have to confirm the number participating? The time that this conversation takes is worth the effort. It is better to wait six months for the event to take place than to rush in and out with something that is not understood or appreciated.

2. Understand the Mission

It is important to identify the connections between the mission of the artists and the school's mission.

The world is full of people who are doing things for others "for their own good." The way to make the arts events work is for everyone—teachers, students, and artists—to perceive that what they are doing is beneficial to them. Common sense dictates: if your project is to integrate experiences of a concert or a museum with the regular music or art instruction, the music or art teachers should help with the planning and assist in developing the repertoire and the instructional materials. Some activities are to promote general cultural awareness. In that case all teachers are more likely to be helpful if they get to participate in a discussion about what these activities might mean to them and their students. If a child asks a teacher, "Why are we going to do this?" the teacher should have a better answer than "I don't know" or "Because it's good for you."

If the arts experience is part of a curriculum unit, the artists need to understand what is in the unit. If the artist is to present a particular point of view about the art form, discuss it in advance. Children do not really like all surprises. They often like to know what is going to happen to them and why. So do adults. Whatever the major purpose may be—to build audiences for the future, to develop writing skills, to develop visual skills, to acquaint children with the contents of a museum, to develop aesthetic judgment—these should be spelled out and agreed to.

3. *Agree on the Objectives of the Program*

All people involved should talk about the main purposes for the activity, i.e. what they are trying to accomplish. That will make it easier to determine which activities to pursue. It will also make it possible to understand each other's mission.

4. *Identify the Age of the Primary Audience*

Projects that are either too mature or too juvenile for students may either frustrate them or bore them. Attention spans vary, capacity to theorize and to think abstractly also varies, as do attitudes toward what is funny, what is embarrassing, what is acceptable, and what is not. In any project it is useful to identify the connections that could exist between the arts activities and the regular school curriculum. Teachers and artists should discuss the activities and share experiences to determine what can work.

Teachers will use materials if they feel they can find something in them that fits in the overall scheme of their teaching. Materials should be intelligent, succinct, interesting, and directed at making the connection for teachers and students. Material that can be passed out to students is especially welcome.

5. *Identify the Teachers Whose Students are Going to Benefit From the Experience*

To accomplish all that is asked of them during a year, teachers plan curricula and school days rather tightly. When teachers are selected—either by their own choice or by recommendations of others—to participate with their students in an arts event, they should be given time to plan the activities that surround it and make the necessary adjustments in other scheduling. Personal conversations with teachers are ideal; discussions at a teachers' meeting is good; written communication is essential.

6. *Understand the Student Audience*

Be sure that anyone who is to lead discussions or do lecture demonstrations for students has some basic skills for doing so. If not, provide them with training and model experiences.

One cannot assume that all people in the arts are going to be effective dealing with children. Some are naturally good teachers. Some are not. Skills can be learned, however, and there are approaches that make some interactions more productive than others. For example, if someone is leading a session in a lecture demonstration where children have a chance to be involved, the speaker should ask open-ended questions that prompt observation and analysis and do not require the children to have a specific answer in mind.

A good type of question for younger students is: "What are some of the things you could say to describe this instrument?" If the children have no ideas, try other questions. "What is it made of? Is that all that it is made of? Look closely. Can you use any words that describe the sound this instrument makes? How is this instrument different from that one?" Wait for a number of answers. If they seem wrong or inappropriate try, "I never thought of that. What makes you say that?"

An unproductive question: "Does anyone know where this instrument is made?" Unless that point has been made on a previous visit, it only prompts random guessing and withdrawal by each child who guesses wrong. Try not to ask questions that have only one answer.

A good type of question for older students: "In the next piece of music you will note that there are three major tempo changes. The music develops as a waltz, a polka, and a march. As we play, listen to the rhythmic beats. See if you can identify the changes and can describe those three types of music."

Or: "In my artwork I try to have a certain kind of subject matter, or shape, or color feeling, or attitude toward materials that drives me. What things do you find in this work? Are there any that are repeated?"

Or: "This dance is based on a theme and variations. Before we begin, listen to the theme played by the clarinet and watch the dancer state the basic theme. As we perform, identify how many different variations you see. Listen for the different ways that the composer varies the theme."

In large groups of students these questions may not be answered during the performance, but students are prompted to listen and watch.

Repetition is important. Rather than cover vast amounts of information, it is more effective to make a few points and make them in different ways. End a session with the question: "Now what did I tell you were the three most important ideas you should consider in seeing these paintings? (or listen to this music, or seeing this play, or watching these dances)."

7. Lay Substantial Groundwork

Make clear statements about the guiding rules of behavior for the events.

Set the ground rules for the events. How much and what kind of student activity is appropriate? If children have never been to a live theater or orchestra performance, they may not realize that their talking can be heard on stage by the performers and that it interrupts the performance. A simple, direct curtain speech that reminds the students of appropriate behavior may be necessary.

If student participation, such as clapping, calling out answers, singing, coming up on stage, volunteering ideas, is wanted, the workshop leader should tell the students what they may do freely. If it is all right to talk while working on an art project, but yelling across the room, leaving the room, or taking extra supplies is not allowed, these rules should be spelled out to the students. Students and non-students accept rules, but they need to know them to comply with them.

8. Keep Promises and Take the Events Seriously

Schools and arts organizations should do what they promised to do. Everyone has a right to expect fully professional behavior from artists and teachers. If a repertoire has been agreed upon, it should not be changed without consultation. If certain classes (grades) are to come at a certain time, that should not be changed. If classroom visits are to be made on a certain schedule, teachers should be ready for the visit and artists should be prepared for their tasks.

Advance materials should be sent on time. Teachers should feel obligated to look at them and use them with their students.

At the same time, flexibility is a great virtue. If a teacher is ill and two classes have to be combined, or if a van breaks down, or if a sprinkler system goes off and forces a change in location, or if the principal gets called to a district emergency meeting, a little humor, good will, and willingness to adjust will keep the project alive for the future.

9. *Manage the Costs Over as Many Units as Possible*

Local fundraising by arts organizations can help sponsor programs. Schools should expect to pay some of the fees as part of their instructional costs. Local arts councils can assist with getting sponsors for educational programming. Sponsors may be as diverse as businesses, band boosters, local arts associations, teachers' unions, local musicians' unions, community foundations, parent-teacher organizations, service clubs, and social clubs. Educational programs can be built into the rehearsal-and-performance schedules of artists in their basic contracts. Intern programs can involve young professionals in the educational program at low cost. Artists series on college campuses bring in artists

who might come to schools for a small additional fee. Faculty in universities, conservatories, art academies, and community college arts programs are frequently available to work with younger students or to offer joint workshops and programming at very low cost. Free-lance artists are often delighted to earn small fees to join with teachers in projects, and their flexibility makes them available for long periods of time. If several schools band together, the costs can be spread among them and minimized.

10. *Commit to Excellence*

Sir Edmund Hillary answered the question "why climb Everest" with the statement "because it is there." To corrupt Sir Edmund Hillary, to decide to climb Mt. Everest you have to know it is there. We seek to be the best only if we have some vision of what is excellent. When we read stories to children, we try to select the works of fine writers. We should show art to children on the same criterion: work provided by fine artists, fine actors, fine musicians. Childhood is not the time to compromise quality. It is the time to set the standard. Work for and with children should be done with care to detail, commitment to artistry, and aesthetic distinction. Work for and with children can be simple, childlike, playful, but it must always be executed with artistic integrity by people who have developed their skills, who are creative, and talented.

When children try their own hands at a new art form they are likely to be clumsy and awkward. They will make unsophisticated choices. Their muscles and minds may be uncoordinated. That is part of the learning process. As they learn to express themselves in an art form, they will also become gradually more and more adept at its technical demands. Their work should not be judged by adult standards, but it can be motivated by the experience of knowing about adult experiences. Children and young people should be able to see what can be achieved in the arts when people work hard at it, when they give themselves to the process, when they study, when they are inspired by creative ideas, when they take risks, try new things, and perfect their art.

It's a clear goal: get the best people available. State and local arts councils will help identify good people. Fellow teachers, faculty in the arts, directors of performing arts series, museum directors, are all potentially good guides. Where possible, see the person's work first. Talk to the arts organization and see if it really cares about work with young people. Read credentials. Call references. Take the time to spend your arts money wisely.

11. *Adapt Good Ideas*

Never hesitate to try something that worked somewhere else, and to modify it to suit your own circumstances. Every idea developed by the twelve organizations described in this book came from a kernel sown somewhere else. The success flowed from plenty of nourishment and attention, a twist of new inspiration, new imagination, extra time taken, or the right pairing of people and places. Ideas are out there.

12. *Commit to the Long Term*

The best interactions between schools and arts organizations are those which occur over time with repeat experiences for all. A few things can be learned on single encounters, but if schools and arts organizations wish to be effective partners, they need to repeat their common efforts, allow opportunities for deepening their understanding of each other and young people. It is important to have a series of activities so children can experiment with their own ideas, make their analyses, and test their thinking. These sustained periods of interaction should balance the temptation to offer "exposure" to a whole list of unconnected things or to a patch-work of audiences.

The 12 organizations discussed in this book worked with schools for six years. During that time many ideas, individuals, and students worked their way through the structure. A commitment to the continuing interaction of the arts with young people was constant, as was a commitment to the continued growth and development of that interaction, and a commitment to the belief that the arts belong in education, and that education is a continuous concern of the arts. This is the partnership that works, over time, to the lasting benefit of the children and the society.

EVALUATION: ASSESSING COLLABORATIVE PROJECTS

... the reason for having begun in the first place.

The topic of evaluation often frightens people in the arts or, at best, suppresses action. It seems contrary to the holistic experience of art to ask questions about the effectiveness of an activity. The fact is, however, people in the arts are constantly making evaluations and changing their work on the basis of judgments. They have so integrated this judgment/alteration process into their work that they do not think of it as evaluation.

It seems fair to assume that a collaborative project between artists and schools has some desired end. It is important for all participants to know if those ends have been achieved. While certain goals are far in the future — helping children discover life-long affinities for participating in the arts — others are more immediate and the success or failure in achieving them can be accounted for. The critical point is to make some effort to discover if the organizations are accomplishing what they set out to do. That means, of course, deciding what those things are, and then deciding what one might accept as evidence of the accomplishment.

Projects have many facets and all of them deserve some attention in an evaluation.

1. Logistics

- How do all parties judge the effectiveness of the staging of events:
- Was the timing right?
- Were the facilities adequate?

- Did everyone know what they needed to know in advance?

2. Quality of the Program

- Was the content appropriate for the age group?
- Were the artists/performers well prepared? Purposeful?
- Did the content of the material capture the interest and imagination of the students?
- Did the content of the program advance the arts experiences of the students beyond their daily routine? How?
- Did the program have any relevance to other work students are doing?
- Did the students seem prepared by the teachers for the event?
- Did the teachers seem supportive of the artists' work?

Questionnaires for teachers and artists can provide a good measure of these factors. Some of the questions need to elicit information beyond a simple yes or no answer. For example:

- What activities did you do with students before the play (concert, museum visit, etc.)?

- What activities did you do with students related to the event after they saw it?
- What would you like to see as the next step in these activities?
- What comments did students make after the workshop?

3. Student Learning

Perhaps this is the most intimidating of the evaluation questions. All teachers ask themselves, "What are the students learning?" Sometimes it seems very difficult to determine. We also know there is much serendipitous learning in any of these encounters with the arts. But just as we would not accept a math or reading program that had no goals for student learning and no checks on that learning, we should not accept an arts program that has no concern for goals in learning. The learning goals may be quite varied, but programs can set some expectations and then can measure them.

What two or three things would you like all students to know or be able to do when this experience has ended?

Examples of Knowing:

- Dance is made up of different kinds of body movements.
- Classical music comes from every country.
- A stringed instrument makes its sound by plucking or bowing.
- A chair can be a work of art.
- Actors create illusions.

Examples of Doing:

- Create dance movement of two different types.
- Clap a variety of rhythms.
- Make a new idea for something to sit on.
- Transform oneself into another character.

Examples of evidence that the students have achieved the goal:

- Students can demonstrate varied dance movements of their own.
- Students can mention some different classical music they have heard and can say what countries the music comes from.
- Students can tell or show how a stringed instrument makes its sound.

- Students can discuss their own ideas about utility, art, and design.
- Students can design their individual interpretations of a chair.
- Students can pretend a situation and create an illusion.

An evaluation of student learning can be as simple as asking students a few questions and noting their responses. If the same questions are asked in much the same way with several groups of children, an informal data base begins to form. The important thing is to keep records. Written questionnaires or quizzes are useful. Oral questionnaires can work effectively.

Certain kinds of learning are revealed in the repeating of an expression, the use of a body or facial gesture, the singing of a melodic phrase, the beating of a rhythm, or the creation of images. Therefore, any testing of student learning needs to be accomplished in several modes that allow for demonstrations beyond those that are verbal. Careful observations of a category of behavior can constitute extremely useful evaluative material. This can be easier than one might think.

For examples:

- Teachers can be asked to note changes in behavior related to the goals of an arts project.
- Rate on a scale of 1-6 (low to high) the accuracy of this statement:

Since we had this workshop:

- Most of my students now use all levels of space (high, medium, and low) when they respond to a creative movement suggestion.
- Most of my students can quickly transform themselves into an imaginative situation and become objects, characters, or creatures with distinctive features.
- My students can improvise dialogue in a creative drama exercise.
- My students have improved in controlling the pitch (bowing, embouchre, fingering, phrasing, etc.) on their instruments.
- My students have become very aware of geometric shapes (line, composition, personal stories, shading, positive/negative space, etc.) in their own artwork.

4. Attitudes of the Students

Some programs are primarily concerned with developing awareness, creating a positive atmosphere for the arts, stimulating creative thinking, and other subtle changes which do not seem easy to measure. Probably the most useful question for project leaders to ask themselves is "What might the children do or say that would indicate this goal had been achieved?"

Examples:

- Students ask to do art work (or to work on their own play, song, or dance).
- Students ask to repeat the arts experience they just had.
  - When will the orchestra come back?
  - When will the players come back?
  - Can we have another master class?
- Students do artwork on their own in their spare time.
- Students seek out arts experiences themselves or with their families.
- Parents ask the school for more arts experiences.
- Other school work shows evidence of the experience.
  - Students write about it, do projects that refer to it.
  - Students talk about it.

To discover if any of this has happened, it will be necessary to make some evaluations several weeks or months after the arts events are concluded. A telephone survey, a questionnaire, or a gathering of participants will be an effective way to discover the success of this aspect of the project.

5. Institutional Strengthening

In the end, arts organizations want to create a healthier environment for the work they do in the arts. Data that indicate numbers of requests for programs, attendance of a target group, income for projects, news coverage, or peer notice should be collected over a period of several years when an arts education program is being planned and implemented. Deal with the question: Is there any change?

At the same time, schools may wish to document changes in curriculum or other program modifications that do or do not occur because of the collaborative arts projects.

- Is there any change in either the general or arts curriculum?

- Have individual teachers made changes in arts-related teaching?
- Is there any change in enrollment in elective arts classes in the junior or senior high school?
- Is there any change in parent interest in the arts in the schools?
- Are there any new student or teacher initiated arts activities in the school?
- Is there any change in the pattern of students choosing arts careers or receiving arts scholarships after graduation?

These data will also need to be collected over several years when a long-term project is the subject.

Some Useful Examples

Artrain came to value the results of systematic evaluation of children's responses to the train's contents. Its staff also collected anecdotal information.

For example, a gallery guide in Charlotte led a dozen groups through the train. The exhibit on Pop Art provided to be a perfect format for discussing how a familiar object — chair, table, silverware — might become a work of art, and what transformations it might undergo at the hands of an artist. The guide later wrote:

"While the children certainly did not seem to have been drilled on these ideas, [the concepts behind Pop Art] in general the students were all able to respond to their embodiment in the works in the gallery. They could describe how familiar things had been changed, could imagine other ways to change them, and were especially interested in how the works of art were made. Predictably, students who had seen the filmstrip had a greater degree of understanding than those who had not [only one of my groups had not] and older children had more sophisticated responses to the works of art. However, I was surprised by how much more responsive and creative the younger students were."

This simple paragraph is an orderly evaluative account of an experience. Had three or four persons done the same thing, one could call it a considered analysis of Artrain's effectiveness. As it stands, it still is very helpful in assessing student responses to their Artrain visit.

A Statewide Evaluation

Because all Michigan Dancers-in-Schools projects were structured similarly, the Michigan Dance Association could conduct a thorough evaluation of its activities across the state. This evaluation documented the effectiveness of the program and indicated the learning that had taken place both with teachers and students. It also demonstrated long-lasting changes resulting from the Dancers-in-Schools program.

The Michigan Dance Association hired a professional evaluator who designed the questionnaires and assured that the returns represented a good sample of teachers involved in the project. The evaluation was intended to discover the degree of participation of teachers, their reaction to the facets of the program, and their use of the ideas subsequent to the residencies.

The findings were:

- 100 percent of the respondents felt the project had achieved its goal;
- 75 percent of the teachers had attended the orientation; and

- 75 percent indicated they had received the written outline.

Of this group 75 percent said the outline was consistent with their present curriculum and slightly over 60 percent attended the concert performance. Those who attended said it was entertaining and designed appropriately, the lectures and classes had made the children receptive to the program, and the program informed staff about dance as an educational experience.

Other findings:

- 68-74 percent said the consultant showed the staff ways to implement movement activities and reinforced academic concepts;
- 50 percent said they had used dance in subsequent instruction; and
- 75 percent said they felt they had learned enough that they *could* use dance in the future.

Of this group 75 percent said that they *would* use it. About 90 percent of the teachers said students benefitted from the project and that the consultants were qualified. When asked to comment on the benefits, they mentioned such things as "creativity...expression... a good break from other activities...a new vocabulary...children feel better about themselves."

The most frequent comment by the teachers when asked for criticism was: "There is not enough of it [the program]."

Taking the Fear Out of Evaluation

Naturally, project planners fear that failure to show positive results can mean the project really isn't working and should be changed. On the other hand, positive evaluation can be wonderfully confirming. Most evaluations reveal both strengths and weaknesses and point the way for repetition and modification.

A negative evaluation can result from attempts to measure the wrong things, or things different from those which the project was expected to accomplish. Therefore, the key to a helpful evaluation is understanding the most valid expectations for the project.

If there are any simple rules, they are:

- Set realistic, understandable goals. Limit their number.
- Agree on realistic, identifiable evidence of their achievement.

- Collect appropriate data/evidence in appropriate modes — written, performed, observed, constructed, drawn and painted, or spoken.
- Analyze data with an understanding of the goals and evidence clearly in mind.
- Record evidence of serendipitous learning, surprises, and other unexpected results.

The whole of these activities will result in an evaluation that informs everyone.

Making it Easy

Another obstacle to evaluation is time. Time is money, and both are usually in short supply. But evaluation can be accomplished as a companion to other project activities.

1. Write Evaluation Questions

Make up short (one page) questionnaires for students, artists, and teachers. A questionnaire can be given to a random sample of students and to all teachers participating in a program. Ask questions whose answers can reveal the attitudes and content for which you are striving. Always solicit open-ended comments because that is often the way people reveal their strongest feelings.

2. Document the Program for Evaluation

Keep a record of the number of students at an event and the number of times these students participated. Have a core list of specific students who have attended a series of events; an evaluator can then interview some of them.

Ask teachers to log observations of a particular behavior such as how often students bring up a topic covered in an arts experience, or how many students have asked to do more of a particular arts activity.

Save samples of student work produced — plays, music, art, or essays.

Make video and audio tapes of activities.

During and immediately after an event, interview a few randomly selected students with a tape recorder. Ask the same question of several students. "What are you doing? What did you just see? What did you learn from going to the museum (concert, play, opera, etc.)?" "Is this the first time you ever saw a live play performed? (heard a concert of a string quartet, watched a person make prints, etc.) Would you like to do this again? Why?"

Give teachers or artists a simple evaluation task. Following a classroom experience with an artist, the teacher or the artist could say: "Everyone take a sheet of paper and write down two things we just did that you thought were interesting." Collect the papers. After a dance specialist has been in a class, the teacher might say: "Everyone on the right side of the room show me a locomotor movement. Everyone on the left side of the room show me a percussive movement." The teacher then makes a note of how many can do it. The task may even be a little written test to see if certain concepts have been learned. "Who wrote this play?" "Match the picture of the instrument with its name." The planners of the collaborative event can prepare these simple follow-up evaluation questions together and give them to the artists and teachers.

3. Analyze the Documents for Their Content

Tabulate ratings on questionnaires and note where the significant numbers of responses lie. In written statements and interviews look for the phrases the students use. Do they mention key ideas or images? Is there any pattern to their responses? In artworks, look for the concepts or gestures that reflect the art experience students have been exposed to. In drama, look for the techniques or imaginative strategies that the resident artist has used. In music, look for the themes, the musical ideas, or the technical expertise stressed in the concert, master class, or performance experience. Remember that at the initial level one expects traces, seeds, references — rather than mastery. Noting how many students have some particular response will be important. Noting what "first timers" say, compared to those who have been to lots of events with their parents, will also be significant. See if students can use the vocabulary from the arts experience in their comments.

Formal evaluations by external reviewers are very helpful once a project has established a record. Many large school districts have professional evaluators on their staff. Smaller districts can go to universities, county educational service agencies, or state educational agencies for help with formal evaluation.

Planning an external evaluation requires a few meetings with the evaluator to help him understand the project and determine the purposes of the evaluation. Professional evaluation is easier to do after three or four years of a project if there has been a record of simple data collection throughout the activities.

Arts organizations and schools can conduct their own evaluation by building upon some of the strategies or questions listed above.

Evaluation can be very revealing. It even can be fun and profitable. A good evaluation is an important factor in requesting funding for future projects. It demonstrates the validity of one's claims. It is essential in designing new and improving old collaborations. No one wants to become obsessed with evaluation; think of it as a persuasive companion to the project's purposes, a guard against stagnation, and a means to find out if all the hard work really made a difference in the students. If not, how can things be set right and made effective? That, after all, is the reason for having begun in the first place.

Project Directory

Mr. Carl Daehler
Director
THE ANN ARBOR CHAMBER
   ORCHESTRA
P.O. Box 7026
Ann Arbor, MI 48107-7026
(313) 996-0066

Total Appropriation: $35,800
Grant Period: 3/1/87 - 2/28/90

Ms. Ann Worth Concannon
Director
ART CENTER OF BATTLE CREEK
265 E. Emmett Street
Battle Creek, MI 49017
(616) 962-9511

Total Appropriation: $159,372
Grant Period: 10/1/86 - 9/30/90

Mr. Daniel E. O'Leary
Director
ARTRAIN, INC.
206 S. Fifth Avenue, Suite 150
Ann Arbor, MI 48104
(313) 662-1293

Total Appropriation: $294,000
Grant Period: 10/1/86 - 9/30/89

Mr. Fritz Stansell
President
BLUE LAKE FINE ARTS CAMP
Route 2
Twin Lake, MI 49457
(616) 894-9026

Total Appropriation: $300,000
Grant Period: 10/1/86 - 9/30/89

Mr. John Peakes
Executive Director
BOARSHEAD THEATER, INC.
425 S. Grand Avenue
Lansing, MI 48933
(517) 484-7800

Total Appropriation: $261,000
Grant Period: 10/1/86 - 9/30/90

Mr. Oleg Lobanov
President
DETROIT SYMPHONY
　ORCHESTRA
Ford Auditorium
Detroit, MI 48226
(313) 567-9000

Total Appropriation: $645,000
Grant Period: 10/1/86 - 9/30/89

Mr. Joseph Bianco, Jr.
Executive Vice President
FOUNDERS SOCIETY DETROIT
INSTITUTE OF ARTS
5200 Woodward Avenue
Detroit, MI 48202
(313) 833-7900

Total Appropriation: $322,500
Grant Period: 9/1/87 - 8/31/90

Mr. Patrick O'Neall
Development Director
THE GRAND RAPIDS
　ORCHESTRA
415 Exhibitors Plaza
Grand Rapids, MI 49503
(616) 454-9451

Total Appropriation: $320,502
Grant Period: 10/1/86 - 9/30/89

Mr. Roger E. Jacobi
President
INTERLOCHEN CENTER FOR
　THE ARTS
Interlochen Arts Academy
Interlochen, MI 49643
(616) 276-9221

Total Appropriation: $309,000
Grant Period: 10/1/86 - 9/30/89

Ms. Jeanette Abeles
Executive Director
MICHIGAN DANCE
　ASSOCIATION
Bailey Community Center
East Lansing, MI 48823
(517) 351-0454

Total Appropriation: $81,000
Grant Period: 10/1/86 - 9/30/89

Dr. David Di Chiera
General Director
MICHIGAN OPERA THEATRE
6519 Second Avenue
Detroit, MI 48202
(313) 874-7850

Total Appropriation: $322,500
Grant Period: 10/1/86 - 9/30/89

Ms. Lavinia Moyer
President/Artistic Director
ROADSIDE ATTRACTIONS,
　INC.
(THE ATTIC THEATRE)
P.O. Box 02457
Detroit, MI 48202
(313) 875-8285

Total Appropriation: $209,703
Grant Period: 10/1/86 - 9/30/89